INSIDE THE
COUNTRY MUSIC HALL OF FAME® AND MUSEUM

A VISITOR'S COMPANION

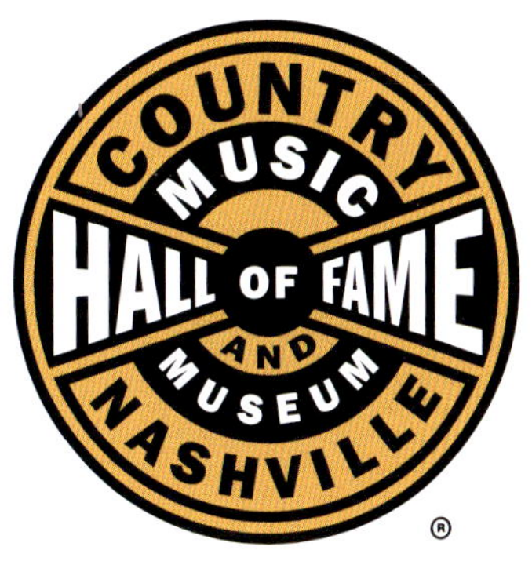

Country Music Foundation Press • 222 Rep. John Lewis Way S • Nashville, Tennessee 37203

 Published 2012, 2015, 2018, 2022, 2024, 2025. Printed in the United States of America.
978-0-915608-49-2

Writers: Michael McCall and Dave Paulson

Editors: Jay Orr and Paul Kingsbury Designers: Margaret Pesek and Roger Blanton

The artifacts, documents, and photographs contained in this book come from the collection of the Country Music Hall of Fame® and Museum.

This project reflects the work of many Country Music Hall of Fame and Museum staff members.
Although space prohibits listing them all, the contributions of CEO Kyle Young, Vice President of Creative Warren Denney, and Vice President of Museum Services Michael Gray deserve special mention.

Photographers Bob Delevante, Marty Stuart, Les Leverett, Donn Jones, david w. clements, and Rick Diamond deserve recognition for their contributions to this book.

CONTENTS

Background: Detail of stage jacket made for Buck Owens by Nudie the Rodeo Tailor.

INTRODUCTION

The Country Music Hall of Fame® and Museum is the world's largest repository of country music artifacts and one of its largest music research centers. This vast collection is presented through dynamic, colorful exhibits featuring one-of-a-kind artifacts and a treasure trove of historic recordings, films, and videos.

The museum's permanent exhibit, *Sing Me Back Home: A Journey Through Country Music*, is divided into two sections: *Sing Me Back Home: The Journey Begins* traces country music from its humble folk roots through its exciting evolution into an internationally recognized commercial art form. *Sing Me Back Home: The Journey Continues* carries the music forward from the 1960s to the artists of today.

The Country Music Hall of Fame and Museum opened in 1967 on Music Row, moved to a new facility in downtown Nashville in 2001, and doubled its space in a 2014 expansion. In 2024, the Museum was honored with a prestigious National Medal of Arts—the highest award given to artists and arts institutions by the United States government.

The museum operates Historic RCA Studio B in partnership with the Mike Curb Family Foundation. The museum also owns Hatch Show Print, one of the oldest active poster print shops in America. Museum offerings include a full menu of live performances and public programs, all contributing to an unforgettable museum experience.

Tuxedo jacket, shirt, and bow tie worn by Jim Reeves.

Western shirt made for Tex Ritter by Nathan Turk, and cowboy hat inscribed from Ritter to Webb Pierce and his wife, Audrey.

THE MUSEUM BUILDING

The Country Music Hall of Fame and Museum's acclaimed building celebrates country music's origins and inspirations through many architectural details.

Viewed from above, the building's outline resembles a massive bass clef. The vertical windows in front are positioned like the black and white keys of a piano, and the dramatic sweep of the building's concrete roofline recalls the tail fin of a late 1950s Cadillac. A replica of the iconic WSM radio tower pierces the roof of the Hall of Fame Rotunda, also evoking a church steeple.

THE ARCHITECTURE

The Hall of Fame Rotunda, with its cylindrical shape, references small-town water towers and grain silos. It is topped by four concentric circles that represent the 78-, 45-, and 33-rpm records and the compact disc. Stone bars on the outside of the Rotunda symbolize the musical notes of the classic Carter Family song "Will the Circle Be Unbroken."

Inside, the Conservatory entrance, bathed in natural light, features a steel frame inspired by the railroads and bridges connecting small-town America. A stream flowing from the second floor to a fountain in the Conservatory represents the movement of music across the American landscape. The floor consists of blocks of southern yellow pine, used in factories and warehouses. Walls of crab orchard stone, from East Tennessee, lend a rustic touch.

In April 2014, the Country Music Hall of Fame and Museum completed a major expansion that includes the Taylor Swift Education Center, the eight-hundred-seat CMA Theater, quarters for historic letterpress company Hatch Show Print, and spectacular gallery and event spaces. The expansion also provided much-needed archival and library storage, to accommodate the materials brought in by the museum's aggressive collecting activity.

EDDY ARNOLD
HAVE YOU SEEN THE SHOW AT THE KNICKERBOCKER THIS WEEK
RIVERSIDE RANCH
TUBB
PEARL

SING ME BACK HOME

THE JOURNEY BEGINS

FOLK ROOTS TO THE 1960s

The museum's permanent exhibit starts with *Sing Me Back Home: The Journey Begins*, a vibrant, multifaceted journey through the first four decades of country music. The exhibit cases illustrate the depth of the museum's archival collection, with one-of-a-kind artifacts collected from the artists who made country music such an integral part of American culture.

Adding to the experience, the museum presents historic photographs, original recordings, archival video and film, interactive media, and beautifully rendered text panels. *Sing Me Back Home* immerses visitors in the history, sights, and sounds of country music through the lives and voices of many of its most beloved personalities.

Custom western-style boots worn by Roy Rogers.

DeFord Bailey

Bradley Kincaid

THE DAWN OF COUNTRY MUSIC

Country music's roots reach into the beginnings of American history. European immigrants brought music with them when they settled in the New World, and so, too, did enslaved West Africans transported there against their will. In the melting pot of America, these various musical strains coalesced to form what came to be known as country music.

As a commercial art form, country music didn't exist until the early twentieth century, when the advent of phonographs and radios allowed vernacular music to be recorded, sold, and broadcast widely. With Thomas Edison's invention of the phonograph in 1877, what started out as the "talking machine" soon became a popular means for musical performances to be captured and eventually packaged and marketed. Sales grew in the early 1900s, after

Harmonica and megaphone used by DeFord Bailey.

Banner promoting Blue Sky Boys performances on radio station WGST, Atlanta.

Left to right: Jimmie Rodgers with the Carter Family: Maybelle Carter, A.P. Carter, Sara Carter, 1931.

Jimmie Rodgers's brakeman's cap and guitar.

recordings evolved from cylinders to discs. By the mid-1920s, companies such as Columbia Phonograph Company and the Victor Talking Machine Company found that recordings with regional sounds and themes became favorites among buyers, and executives at the record companies began traveling the rural South to find homegrown performers.

Radio stations proliferated across America after 1920, becoming a major outlet for musical performances. As on recordings, music with rustic overtones proved popular on the airwaves. Country musicians first performed on radio in 1922, and, within a few years, radio stations initiated the first barn dances—ensemble variety programs with the relaxed, chatty atmosphere of a family gathering. Such down-home shows drew rural audiences as well as city dwellers attracted to the old-fashioned way of life the barn-dance programs recalled.

Left: Ernest "Pop" Stoneman's autoharp, with carrying case designed to act as an amplifier when the autoharp was placed on the case.

Below and right: Fiddle used by Fiddlin' John Carson, and handpainted acoustic guitar played by his daughter and performing partner, Moonshine Kate.

Pop Stoneman

Radio stations in Chicago, Nashville, and other cities soon launched their own barn dances, attracting loyal fans and advertisers. Regional and national businesses, eager to associate their products with the traditional themes of these shows, lined up to sign on as sponsors. Thanks to the spread of rustic programs, country entertainers got more work and greater exposure, making them a vital part of listeners' lives.

Audience members attached themselves to favorite performers, and the first country stars emerged, including Jimmie Rodgers, the Carter Family, Uncle Dave Macon, and Vernon Dalhart.

Through the twentieth century, even as technologies changed, country music would continue to find favor with the public via recordings and radio airplay—much as it had in its very earliest days.

Blue Sky Boys

Mandolin and guitar used by the Blue Sky Boys, Bill (mandolin) and Earl Bolick.

Bonnie Dodd

Fiddlin' John Carson and Moonshine Kate

Paul Warmack's Gully Jumpers.
Left to right: Bert Hutcherson, Roy Hardison, Charley Arrington, and Paul Warmack.

Paul Warmack's guitar.

Bonnie Dodd's
National resonator guitar.

THE PRECIOUS JEWEL

A select few musical instruments have become country music icons. The music fashioned on them helped shape American culture.

JIMMIE RODGERS'S MARTIN 00-18

On August 4, 1927, at a makeshift studio in a former furniture store in Bristol, on the Virginia-Tennessee border, an unknown singer from Mississippi made his first recordings for Victor Records. Accompanying himself on this plain-looking but elegantly designed mahogany and spruce Martin 00-18 guitar. Jimmie Rodgers recorded two songs that day, "The Soldier's Sweetheart" and "Sleep Baby Sleep." Released two months later, they launched a recording career that would turn him into country music's first superstar.

The inscription "8-4-27 B. VA-TENN," written in India ink inside the guitar's sound hole, documents Rodgers's recording debut at the Bristol Sessions, which marked a turning point in the history of country music.

These treasures are currently displayed as part of the museum's collection—and serve as enduring symbols of the power of music.

MAYBELLE CARTER'S 1928 GIBSON L-5 GUITAR

In 1928, with money from the Carter Family's successful first recordings, nineteen-year-old Maybelle Carter paid $275 for the finest guitar she could find, a 1928 Gibson L-5 model. Until her death in 1978, "Mother Maybelle" used it on hundreds of recordings, radio and television programs, and live appearances.

As the first f-hole, arch-top guitar, the L-5 was designed to be twice as loud as any flat-top guitar of the period. Carter used it to revolutionize the role of the guitar, transforming the rhythm instrument into a distinctive lead voice. Her signature "Carter scratch"—heard on classics such as "Keep on the Sunny Side" and "Wildwood Flower"—became the most imitated guitar style in America during the 1920s and 1930s.

STEEL GUITAR RAG

STYLISTIC INNOVATIONS

Country music in the 1920s and 1930s benefited from an exciting infusion of regional diversity. Country's principal sound remained that of fiddle-driven stringbands, but some groups began incorporating pop and jazz influences that broadened the music's possibilities.

In Chicago, the Prairie Ramblers (which included singer Patsy Montana) injected swing and cowboy music into their repertoire while dressing in western outfits.

In the Southwest, fiddle-band veterans such as Milton Brown drew inspiration from jazz and blues to create western swing. In Louisiana, the Hackberry Ramblers merged Cajun fiddle music with country music, eventually growing into a full-fledged Louisiana swing band, complete with horns and drums.

Hackberry Ramblers

Milton Brown & His Musical Brownies

Guitar and custom-painted drum played by members of the Hackberry Ramblers.

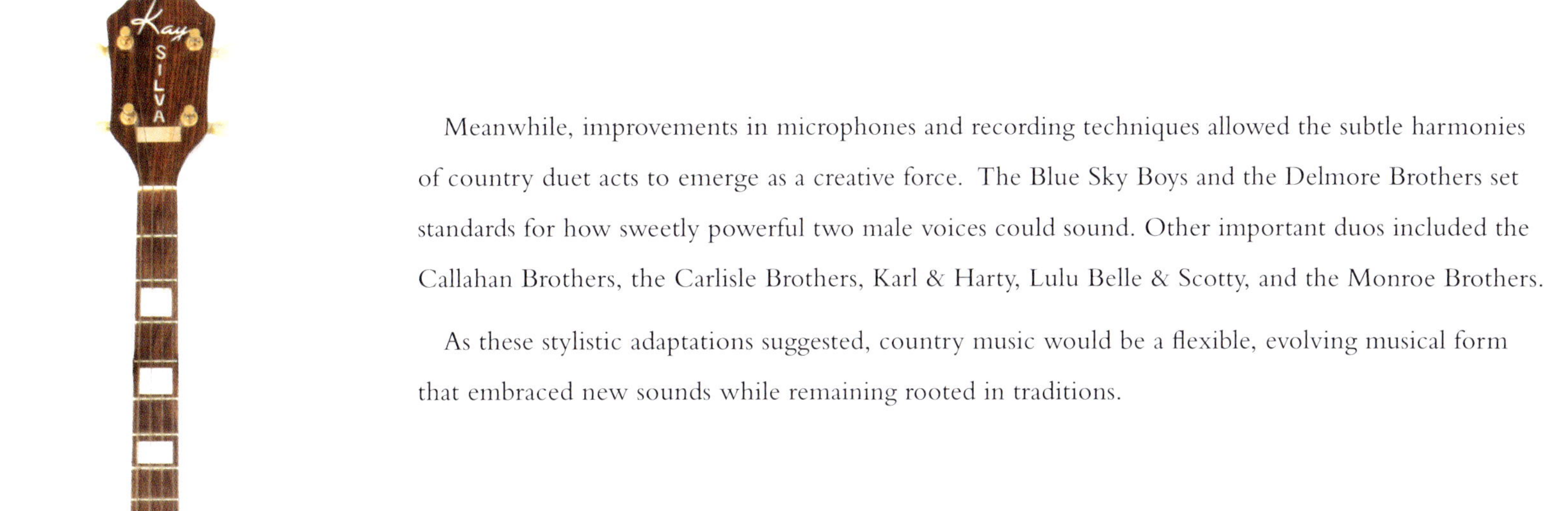

Meanwhile, improvements in microphones and recording techniques allowed the subtle harmonies of country duet acts to emerge as a creative force. The Blue Sky Boys and the Delmore Brothers set standards for how sweetly powerful two male voices could sound. Other important duos included the Callahan Brothers, the Carlisle Brothers, Karl & Harty, Lulu Belle & Scotty, and the Monroe Brothers.

As these stylistic adaptations suggested, country music would be a flexible, evolving musical form that embraced new sounds while remaining rooted in traditions.

Prairie Ramblers with Patsy Montana

Rabon and Alton Delmore

Left: Tenor banjo played by Chick Hurt of the Prairie Ramblers.

Right: Western boots worn by Chick Hurt of the Prairie Ramblers.

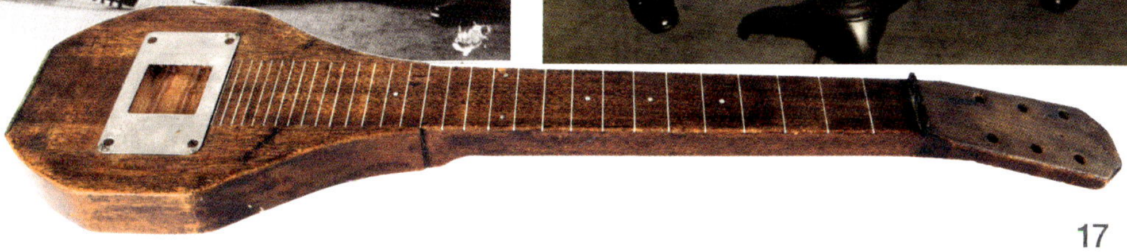

Far Right: Lap steel used by Bob Dunn of Milton Brown & His Musical Brownies.

Carl T. Sprague

Patsy Montana

BACK IN THE SADDLE

THE WESTERN INFLUENCE

In American mythology, the cowboy represents bravery, romance, and self-sufficiency. No wonder that musically diverse country entertainers, seeking a visual style that spoke of heartland values, adopted the western look.

Jimmie Rodgers, one of country music's first national stars, sometimes wore broad-brimmed cowboy hats and leather chaps for publicity photos. Rodgers acolytes Ernest Tubb, Hank Williams, and Hank Snow would adopt their own versions of western costuming.

In the 1930s, Carl T. Sprague recorded authentic western songs he learned while herding cattle in Texas. Around the same time, Gene Autry became a star on Chicago radio station WLS before moving to

Left: Detail of artwork on the back of Carl T. Sprague's resonator guitar.

Right: Patsy Montana's western boots, which she designed.

Below: Tex Ritter's Colt single-action revolver.

Gene Autry

Roy Rogers

Tex Ritter

Los Angeles in 1934. His appearance in the 1934 Republic Pictures film *In Old Santa Fe* launched one of the era's most successful film-acting careers; the down-home warmth of Autry's baritone voice and the humble heroism of his screen character proved reassuring to Depression Era audiences.

Tex Ritter, a Lone Star state native, played cowboys in Broadway musicals and on radio shows before starring in his first western film in 1936. In the 1940s, Roy Rogers emerged as the most successful film cowboy since Autry. Born Leonard Slye, Rogers was given his screen name by Hollywood. In 1947, he married his most popular co-star, Dale Evans, and the two later starred in a TV series, *The Roy Rogers Show.*

Marty Robbins, Willie Nelson, George Strait, and Garth Brooks are among other stars who have shown a cowboy influence. Like a good country song, the western look is intrinsically American—and suggests that certain values remain strong no matter what else goes on in the world.

Top right: Poster promoting Trail to San Antone, *starring Gene Autry.*

Right: Dale Evans's boots, and plastic figurine of Roy Rogers on his horse, Trigger.

Detail of accordion played by Pee Wee King.

TENNESSEE SATURDAY NIGHT

NASHVILLE TAKES THE LEAD

By the 1940s, Nashville was fast becoming the capital of country music. The Grand Ole Opry gained in national prominence when the NBC Radio Network began broadcasting a half-hour of the program on Saturday evenings in October 1939. By the mid-1940s, this popular segment, sponsored by Prince Albert Smoking Tobacco, helped transform the Opry from one of many regionally popular barn dances into a nationally known radio program with a reputation for cultivating country music stars.

In 1943, the Opry's popularity led to a move to the Ryman Auditorium on Fifth Avenue in downtown Nashville, allowing for larger audiences at its live weekly program. Each Saturday night, the Ryman hosted two audiences of some 2,000 persons each, many of whom came from different states.

Pee Wee King's accordion.

Roy Acuff's fiddle.

Minnie Pearl

Roy Acuff

Poster for the 1950 movie Hoedown, *featuring Eddy Arnold.*

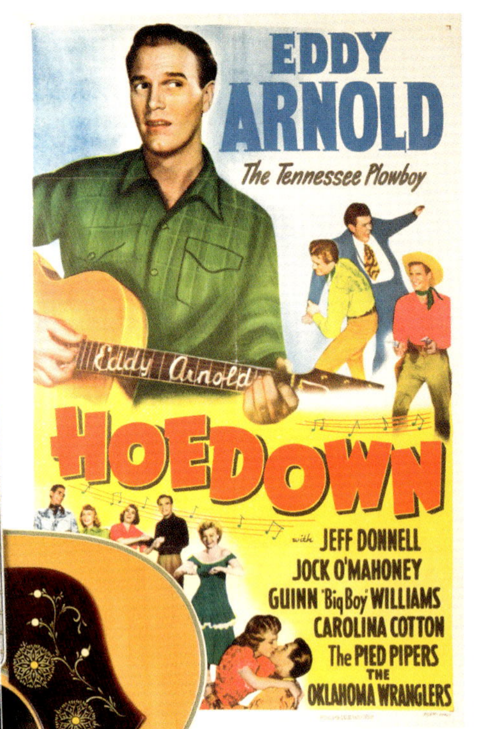

Dress and hat worn by Minnie Pearl during appearances on the Grand Ole Opry.

The Opry cast members who became national stars in the 1940s included Roy Acuff, Eddy Arnold, Red Foley, Pee Wee King, Bill Monroe, Minnie Pearl, and Ernest Tubb. As more stars emerged from Nashville, the city began growing into a recording and music-business center.

Acuff and songwriter Fred Rose formed the music publishing firm Acuff-Rose Publications in 1942, making it one of the first prominent music companies in town. Two years later, Eddy Arnold successfully cut a hit record in Nashville, and subsequently the city's reputation as a recording hub grew, drawing more attention and investment from major record labels headquartered in New York and Los Angeles.

Right: Cotton bag for Roy Acuff's Own Flour, sold in the 1940s. The bag included a Roy Acuff doll that could be cut out, sewn, and stuffed.

Left: Eddy Arnold's 1967 Gibson J-200N guitar, an almost exact reproduction of his 1948 Gibson SJ-200.

Hank Williams's suit and western boots, made by Nudie the Rodeo Tailor.

In 1946, Fred Rose began working with Hank Williams, then a young, little-known songwriter and performer residing in Montgomery, Alabama. By 1947, Rose had secured Williams a record contract and had begun producing his recordings. Two years later, when Williams achieved his first #1 hit, "Lovesick Blues," the lanky Alabama singer left the *Louisiana Hayride* barn dance in Shreveport to accept an invitation to join the Grand Ole Opry, moving to Nashville with his wife and newborn son.

The national impact Williams had as a recording artist and a touring member of the Opry heightened the prominence of the radio show and Nashville as the place many aspiring country artists, musicians, and songwriters wanted to be. Soon, the music industry bloomed around all the talent moving to Middle Tennessee.

Pee Wee King

Eddy Arnold

Hank Williams

THE PRECIOUS JEWEL

A select few musical instruments have become country music icons. The music fashioned on them helped shape American culture.

HANK WILLIAMS'S MARTIN D-28

Hank Williams used this 1944 Martin D-28 guitar to create his unsurpassed legacy as a country singer and songwriter. Among the instruments he owned, this is regarded as his finest. The scratches on its top reflect the wear and tear of countless personal appearances made by the charismatic Williams, everywhere from nightclubs and outdoor concerts to national television.

After Williams's tragic death at age twenty-nine, on New Year's Day, 1953, the guitar passed into the possession of his family. It was handed down to Hank Williams Jr., who kept alive the family tradition by using it occasionally in performance. Hank Jr. preserved the guitar for the most part as his father had left it, with its original herringbone purfling, ebony fretboard with slotted diamond-shaped inlays, and wartime-style tuners with white, plastic buttons.

These treasures are currently displayed as part of the museum's collection—and serve as enduring symbols of the power of music.

BILL MONROE'S 1923 GIBSON F-5 MANDOLIN

The most famous mandolin in American music history, Bill Monroe's Gibson F-5 Master Model is one of the finest stringed instruments ever made.

Monroe bought the instrument in the early 1940s, when he spotted it in a Florida barbershop window. It became his second voice, filling in around his high, lonesome singing and ringing out during the supercharged solos that were a hallmark of his aggressive playing style.

In 1985, an intruder broke into Monroe's home and smashed the treasured mandolin with a fireplace poker. The instrument was painstakingly reconstructed by Gibson's Charlie Derrington from about 150 slivers of broken wood, and it remained Monroe's constant companion, onstage and in the recording studio, for the rest of his life.

Detail of Cindy Walker's Royal typewriter.

HOLLYWOOD BARN DANCE

COUNTRY MOVES WEST

Among the Dust Bowl images imprinted on history are cars crammed full of rural migrants and their family belongings. Often, the baggage included a musical instrument—a visual reminder that those on the move carried their music with them to California.

Indeed, Los Angeles, Bakersfield, and other California cities became country music outposts largely because working-class Americans brought in honky-tonk, western swing, and other country styles. Soon, country sounds filled dance halls, radio programs, and recording studios, and performers like Bob Wills & His Texas Playboys, Spade Cooley, Hank Thompson, and Merle Travis went there to advance their influential careers.

Right: Custom-painted Royal typewriter used by Cindy Walker to compose her hit songs.

Below: Bob Wills's inlaid fiddle.

Bob Wills

Cindy Walker

Merle Travis

T. Texas Tyler

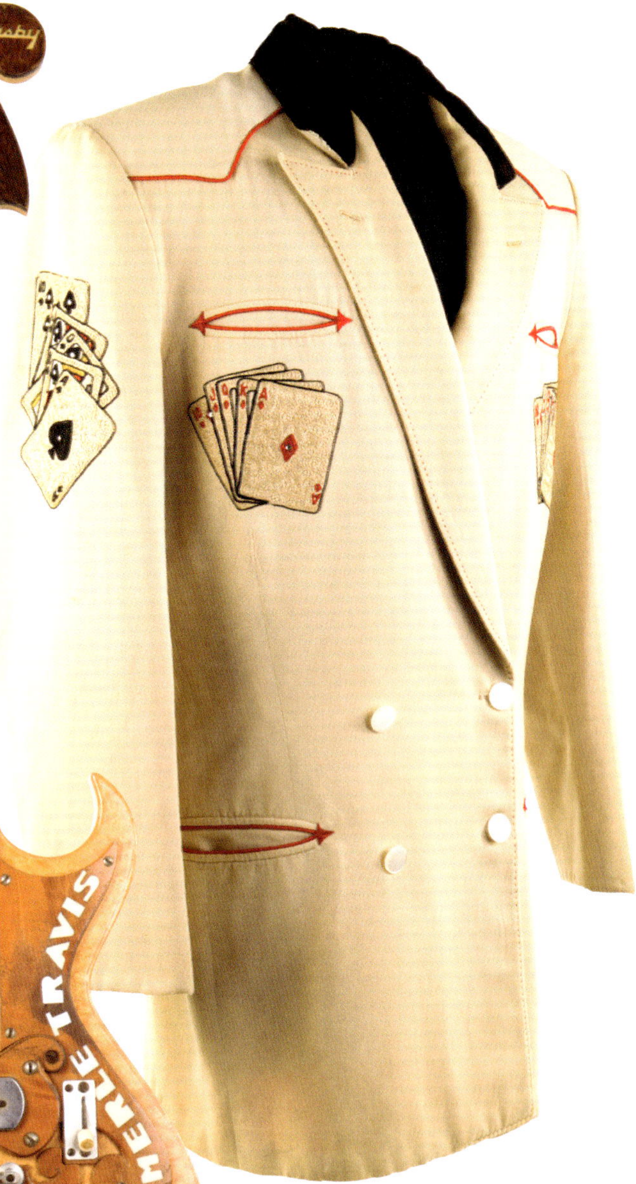

From Long Beach in the south to Oakland in the north—two cities that lured workers to defense-industry jobs during World War II—western swing bands led by Wills and Cooley attracted crowds competing in number with those of swing-era giants Tommy Dorsey and Benny Goodman.

Wills already was a star in Texas and Oklahoma when, in 1943, he returned from military service in World War II and relocated his band, the Texas Playboys, from Tulsa to Los Angeles. The charismatic, cigar-chomping fiddler proved his instincts were right, as he became one of the nation's highest-paid bandleaders. Wills also recorded some of his best-loved hits during this period, including "Roly Poly" (1946). Like Wills, Cooley and his band played popular swing-shift dances, staging late-night shows for those who got off work after midnight. His broad-based popularity and the expertise of his band led to his first #1 hit, "Shame on You," in 1945.

Above: T. Texas Tyler's suit jacket, made by Nudie the Rodeo Tailor.

Left: Merle Travis's Bigsby guitar.

Meanwhile, perceptive songwriters such as Cindy Walker also succeeded in California's vibrant country community. Walker provided a bounty of songs for Wills, including "Cherokee Maiden" and "Bubbles in My Beer," as well as writing songs for westerns (Gene Autry's hit "Blue Canadian Rockies") and other Hollywood films. Walker's career extended for decades, encompassing such classics as Ernest Tubb's "Warm Red Wine," Eddy Arnold's "You Don't Know Me" (also a hit for Ray Charles), and Roy Orbison's "Dream Baby (How Long Must I Dream)."

During the 1950s and 1960s, Los Angeles and Bakersfield joined Nashville as country music centers, with Buck Owens, Merle Haggard, Glen Campbell, and Dwight Yoakam among those who continued that legacy. Their success proved that country music's popularity knew no geographic boundaries.

Hank Thompson

Cliffie Stone

Above: Hank Thompson's leather stage jacket made by Nudie the Rodeo Tailor.

Left: Cliffie Stone owned and played this unusual triple-neck guitar on the Hometown Jamboree *TV show he created and hosted in Southern California. The guitar was originally owned by Stone's father, Herman Snyder, who played in Stuart Hamblen's band and on his West Coast radio shows.*

SETTIN' THE WOODS ON FIRE

NEW SOUNDS ON THE JUKEBOX

As country music expanded from coast to coast, the southern regions where it first came to life continued to develop new ways to energize the genre to fit the times. In the 1940s, two new sounds surfaced, one born of urban nightspots and rural roadhouses, the other bringing instrumental fire and vocal splendor to traditional string music.

As performers began appearing in rough-and-tumble clubs, they created by necessity a louder, amplified musical style driven by keening fiddles, electric guitars, and steel guitars; it became known as honky-tonk. Meanwhile, a willful Kentucky mandolinist, Bill Monroe, forged a dynamic stringband sound emphasizing the banjo, fiddle, and

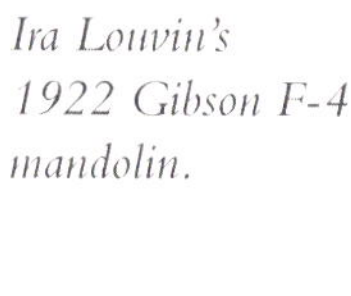

Ira Louvin's 1922 Gibson F-4 mandolin.

Lester Flatt and Earl Scruggs

Ira and Charlie Louvin

Detail of Lefty Frizzell's stage costume, designed by Nudie the Rodeo Tailor.

harmony vocals as well as his own virtuoso mandolin work. This new genre would be named bluegrass, after Monroe's band, the Blue Grass Boys.

Honky-tonk appealed to young people who left their "home out on the rural route," as Hank Williams sang, and to hard-working folks who wanted to blow off steam. Played on electrified instruments with enough volume to be heard over a rowdy crowd, honky-tonk songs dealt with loss, spiritual desolation, and the difficulties of relationships in a time of change. These songs also celebrated stepping out on Saturday night and the temptations of the evening.

Bluegrass emerged during this same period, a rhythmically driven style rooted in the conservative morals of family and religion. Tightly arranged and played with propulsive precision, the music challenged instrumentalists to reach new heights. Monroe and banjoist Earl Scruggs pushed the music forward with virtuosity and vision, creating an aesthetically adventurous sound still grounded in tradition.

Left: Carter Stanley's customized 1958 Martin D-28 guitar.
Below: Gibson RB-2 banjo owned by Ralph Stanley.

Personalized western boots worn by Lefty Frizzell, designed by Nudie the Rodeo Tailor.

Hank Snow

Carter and Ralph Stanley

Lefty Frizzell

The music created by Monroe and Flatt & Scruggs inspired generations of vocalists and musicians. Both the Stanley Brothers and the Louvin Brothers explored the power of sky-high harmonies and stripped-down acoustic arrangements, with the former emerging as bluegrass stalwarts and the latter growing into an influential country and gospel act.

Honky-tonk would prove similarly flexible. Practitioners such as Hank Snow opened it up to include blues, Hawaiian music, and Latin influences, while stylists like Lefty Frizzell proved the music could include sentimentality and humor, with Frizzell's note-bending vocals exerting a strong influence on artists such as George Jones, Merle Haggard, John Anderson, Randy Travis, Keith Whitley, and Alan Jackson.

Hank Snow's stage costume, created by Nudie the Rodeo Tailor, based on Snow's hit song "Golden Rocket."

Elvis Presley

The Everly Brothers at RCA Studio B.

LET'S HAVE A PARTY

REAL GONE COUNTRY

When rock & roll stomped, swiveled, and shook its way onto the American cultural scene, it rattled the entire music industry. The music's youth appeal cut into country music's popularity and sales, and it influenced Nashville's future in several ways.

But country music played a direct role in rock & roll's birth. Nearly all of the groundbreaking songs created at Sun Studios in Memphis—an early epicenter of rock & roll—drew on country traditions and Beale Street blues.

Elvis Presley made that connection explicit with his first single, a cover of bluesman Arthur Crudup's "That's All Right" as the A-side, and a sped-up version of bluegrass pioneer Bill Monroe's "Blue Moon of Kentucky" as its B-side. The coupling illustrated how this brash new sound married blues and country traditions, energized by youthful abandon.

Carl Perkins's blue suede shoes.

Carl Perkins and his band.
Left to right: Clayton Perkins, Carl Perkins, W.S. Holland, and Jay Perkins.

All of Sun Records' renowned rock & rollers came from poor, rural, southern backgrounds, and they grew up worshipping the Grand Ole Opry. Yet Jerry Lee Lewis, Carl Perkins, Johnny Cash, and Charlie Rich likely wouldn't have received recording contracts in Nashville—even though all of them were sooner or later embraced by country fans. It took a record label willing to gamble on an impetuous new sound for rock & roll to grow into a national phenomenon.

Of course, some country musicians drew inspiration from rock & roll, too, as heard in Marty Robbins's "Ruby Ann" and Sonny James's "Young Love." As country singer Bob Luman said, after hearing Elvis Presley in concert, "That's the last time I tried to sing like Webb Pierce or Lefty Frizzell."

Left: Stage costume shirt worn by Jerry Lee Lewis.

Right: Leather jackets worn by Don Everly (right) and Phil Everly (left).

Jerry Lee Lewis

Brenda Lee

Wanda Jackson

Indeed, a generation of rockabilly artists heated up the airwaves with a wild blend of hillbilly music and rock & roll attitude. One of the best-known rockabilly songs of the 1950s, "Blue Suede Shoes," came from Carl Perkins, a former field worker from Tiptonville, Tennessee, who cited the Opry and music he heard from Black sharecroppers as the primary sources of his sound.

Nashville also recorded rock & roll hits, with the Everly Brothers (backed by Chet Atkins), Brenda Lee (produced by Owen Bradley), and Roy Orbison (produced by Fred Foster) among the best-known stars in Nashville's rock countdown. Elvis, after leaving Sun Records for RCA, recorded many classic hits at RCA Studio B, in the heart of what would become Nashville's Music Row neighborhood.

Wanda Jackson's 1959 Martin D-28 guitar and fringed stage costume.

Patsy Cline

SWEET DREAMS

THE NASHVILLE SOUND

Nashville responded to rock & roll by evolving toward a more cosmopolitan sound. In Music Row studios, fiddles and steel guitars gave way to lush orchestrations and honeyed harmonies. Producers Chet Atkins and Owen Bradley relied on skilled studio musicians—the "A Team"—whose creative input and quick adaptability made them vital to the hit-making process.

The appealing style they created became known as the Nashville Sound. It included vocalists Patsy Cline and Jim Reeves, whose rich tones and clear enunciation worked well with sophisticated arrangements. Imaginative singer-songwriters like Don Gibson benefited from modern sounds that focused attention on their inventive wordplay.

Jim Reeves

Cufflinks, button covers, and red patent leather shoes worn by Jim Reeves.

Cocktail gown worn by Patsy Cline.

A few Nashville veterans adapted well to the polished production style. Eddy Arnold, Ray Price, and Marty Robbins found that their voices blended well with urbane flourishes. Similarly, female singers Skeeter Davis and Dottie West created enduring recordings that brought new listeners to country music.

Meanwhile, the Country Music Association, formed in 1958, marshaled the industry's forces to more actively promote its songs and stars to radio stations, the media, and advertisers. Suddenly, the popular appeal of country music became more visible, leading to more growth.

Some country traditionalists balked at such moves, complaining that the uptown sounds took country music too far from its down-home roots. But Nashville continued to present artists with traditional styles alongside the sweetened productions of some of its stars.

Country music has always been a big-tent genre that responds to changes in popular culture by bringing in new influences. The Nashville Sound was a reaction to its times—as well as another step in the genre's ongoing evolution.

Marty Robbins

Don Gibson

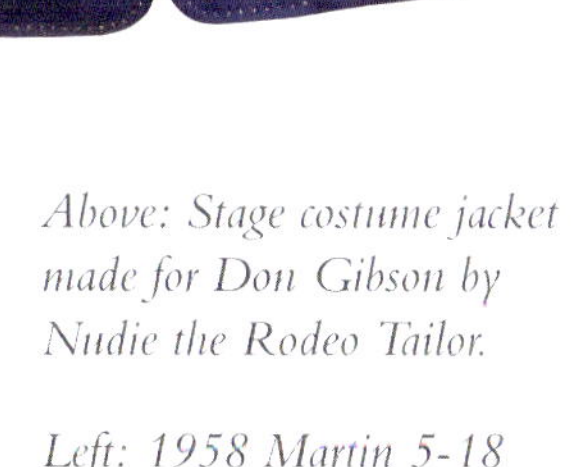

Above: Stage costume jacket made for Don Gibson by Nudie the Rodeo Tailor.

Left: 1958 Martin 5-18 guitar, played by Marty Robbins.

WEBB PIERCE'S 1962 PONTIAC BONNEVILLE

Some entertainers enjoyed custom-designed cars as flashy as their stage wear.

Webb Pierce's 1962 Pontiac Bonneville features ornamental pistols and rifles on the hood and handles, horseshoes for pedals, and more than a thousand silver dollars in the tooled-leather upholstery. A mock saddle serves as the console between the front bucket seats.

Western fashion kingpin Nudie the Rodeo Tailor, a favorite of country stars, custom-designed the Pontiac. Six were built, each with a selling price of $20,000, a goodly sum in the early 1960s.

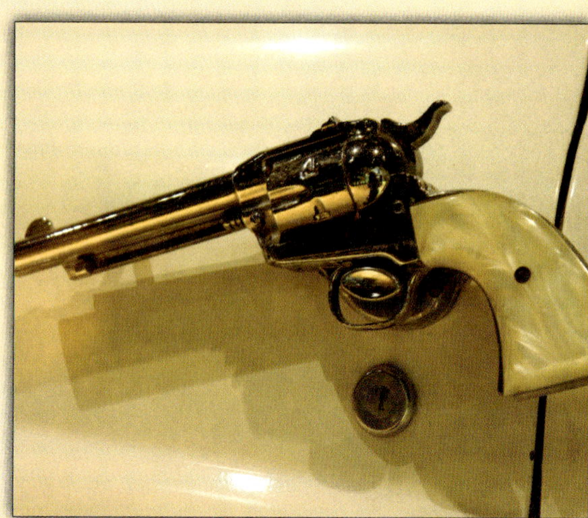

ELVIS PRESLEY'S 1960 CADILLAC LIMOUSINE

Elvis Presley's 1960 Cadillac limousine includes gold-plated highlights and forty coats of paint containing crushed diamonds and fish scales.

The luxurious back seat features a small television console with an antenna for reception, a state-of-the-art stereo system complete with a record player operated by the rear passengers, an early version of a car phone, and a communication system so those in back could talk with the driver.

The car was customized specifically for Presley by Barris Kustom City of North Hollywood, with Presley personally involved in its design.

Ray Price

Charley Pride

SWINGING DOORS

THE RETURN OF HARD COUNTRY

Not everyone in the country music industry believed that rock & roll drowned out the appeal of straight-up country music. Indeed, many performers seized the moment to enliven old-school, fiddle-and-steel sounds with inventive rhythms, piercing harmonies, and memorable songwriting.

Ray Price, for one, juiced Texas honky-tonk with a catchy shuffle beat and western swing-style soloing. He employed a four-four rhythm reinforced by drums and special walking bass lines, providing a dance-floor foundation for jazzy fiddle and steel runs and Price's soaring voice. With two-stepping specialties like "Crazy Arms" and "City Lights," Price combined honky-tonk and swing into a fresh, energized sound that inspired generations of artists and fans.

Meanwhile, the oil-and-agriculture town of Bakersfield, California, became home to a stripped-down country sound that captured the attention of many transplanted Americans chased west by Depression Era dust storms.

Buck Owens and his band, the Buckaroos, fashioned a hot country sound that took rock's energy and filtered it through

Ray Price's stage jacket, created by Nudie the Rodeo Tailor.

Personalized label sewn into the lining of Ray Price's stage jacket.

a country sensibility packed with loads of personality and talent. By the mid-1960s, Owens hits such as "Tiger by the Tail" and "Act Naturally" firmly established his music as a counterpoint to the smooth Nashville Sound.

Bakersfield soon produced another Country Music Hall of Fame member when Merle Haggard swaggered forth with fiercely concise barroom music buoyed by heartfelt songs torn from his wayward youth, his personal struggles, and his views on American society.

Nashville served up its share of tradition-leaning country stars as well. Faron Young packed a punch with honky-tonk songs that filled a vacuum left by the death of his hero, Hank Williams. The raucous 1955 hit "Live Fast, Love Hard, Die Young," Young's first #1, proved that Music City still produced songs with rough edges.

Above: Detail of Merle Haggard's pardon, signed by then-governor of California, Ronald Reagan.

Left: Buck Owens's signature guitar.

Buck Owens & the Buckaroos.
Left to right: Don Rich, Willie Cantu, Buck Owens, Tom Brumley, and Doyle Holly.

Merle Haggard

Faron Young

Connie Smith

Connie Smith, a reserved young family woman from Ohio, hit #1 with her first release, "Once a Day," announcing herself as one of the great traditional singers of her era. Arriving in Nashville amid the Civil Rights Era, Charley Pride established his traditional country bona fides with a deep, down-home voice that made him one of the most popular old-school singers of his generation. Both Smith and Pride would endure for decades, proudly carrying their traditional country sounds into the twenty-first century, to the delight of country fans worldwide.

Left: Connie Smith's 1968 Gibson Dove guitar.

Right: Custom guitar built for Faron Young by Canadian luthier Frank Gay.

Upper Right: Faron Young's fringed suede jacket.

Detail from stage costume designed for Hank Snow.

NUDIE THE RODEO TAILOR

Nudie Cohn brought flash and sparkle to western-wear costumes, a look that became synonymous with country music from the 1940s through the 1960s. Setting up shop in Hollywood as Nudie the Rodeo Tailor, Cohn created custom-designed stagewear for everyone from Gene Autry and Hank Williams to Elvis Presley and Gram Parsons.

Clothing label for Nudie's Rodeo Tailors.

Cover of catalog for Nudie's Rodeo Tailors.

Left: Boots created for Hank Thompson, based on his song "Humpty Dumpty Heart."

Below: Stage costume created for Merle Haggard, early 1970s.

Above: Stage costume designed for Lefty Frizzell.

NATHAN TURK

From the 1930s to the 1970s, western-wear designer Nathan Turk created lavishly embroidered stage costumes for country singers and celluloid cowboys. His clients included the Maddox Brothers & Rose, who earned billing as "the most colorful hillbilly band in the land." Other regular customers included Roy Rogers, Hank Snow, Hank Thompson, and Ernest Tubb.

Above: Nathan Turk clothing label.

Far left: Stage costume worn by Fred Maddox.

Left: Stage costume designed for Buck Owens and worn onstage at his 1966 Carnegie Hall concert.

Right: Stagewear designed for Rose Maddox.

Detail of stage costume worn by Don Maddox.

Judy and Steve Turner GALLERIES
SING ME BACK HOME
THE
JOURNEY
CONTINUES
1960s TO THE PRESENT

NASHVILLE REBELS

SING ME BACK HOME

THE JOURNEY CONTINUES

1960s TO THE PRESENT

By the 1960s, country music was an established American art form. Mirroring American life, the music of the ensuing decades included experimentation, fragmentation, resolve, a longing for tradition, and a race to keep up with technological advances.

As with society at large, the world of country music experienced highs and lows. But the right songs always surfaced to keep country music relevant and entertaining. The music communicated what changed about America—and what stayed the same. Country songs continued to address the trials, the triumphs, and the yearning for freedom, for love, for family, for community, and for the right to pursue the American dream.

Brad Paisley's first electric guitar, a Sears Silvertone, with amplifier and speaker built into the guitar case.

Ray Charles

Roger Miller

WHEN TWO WORLDS COLLIDE

COUNTRY MEETS MASS MARKET

By the mid-1960s, a new crop of talent made it clear country music would continue to flourish despite the loss of younger listeners to the rise of rock & roll. Thanks to several distinctly gifted performers, country made inroads into the mainstream of American culture in ways it hadn't in previous decades.

For example, R&B titan Ray Charles's 1962 album *Modern Sounds in Country and Western Music* re-imagined classic country songs as lush, soulful ballads and brassy uptempo numbers. His take on Don Gibson's soaring song "I Can't Stop Loving You" spent five weeks at #1 on the *Billboard* pop charts.

Roger Miller brought an air of hipster élan to his imaginative brand of country music. Songs such as "King of the Road," "Chug-a-Lug," and "Dang Me" were unlike anything before them, using unusual yet infectious arrangements that matched Miller's clever wordplay and his skewed perspective on society.

Below: Ray Charles's sunglasses.

Right: Roger Miller's 1963 Gibson C-1E Classic nylon-string guitar.

Opposite page: John Hartford's song manuscript for "Gentle on My Mind."

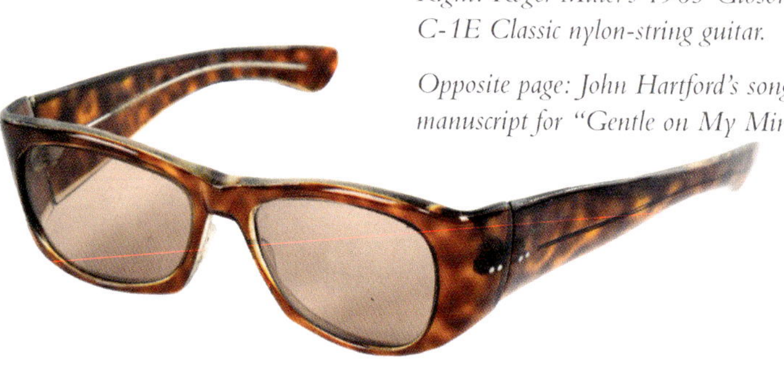

SOUP BACK FROM A GU
CRACKLIN' CAULDRON IN SOME
MY BEARD & ROUGHENING COAL PILE &
HAT PULLED LOW ACROSS M
THROUGH CUPPED HANDS 'ROUND A TIN
PRETEND TO HOLD YOU TO MY BRE
THAT YOU'RE MOVING ON THE BACKROADS BY T
MEMORY AND FOREVER YOU'RE THE RIVER
GENTLE ON MY MIND

Tho the wheat fields clothe
And junkyards & hways come b
Some other woman cryin to
'll mother cause she turn
might run in s
might st
sugar

Jeannie Seely moved from Los Angeles to Nashville in 1965 to pursue a singing career. Less than a year later, she was a star, thanks to the Grammy-winning hit "Don't Touch Me." Its sensual lyrics ruffled some feathers—as did Seely's decision to wear miniskirts on the Grand Ole Opry.

Arkansas native Glen Campbell became a star thanks to hosting a popular network TV show, *The Glen Campbell Goodtime Hour*, and issued a series of imaginative story songs, including "Gentle on My Mind" and "Wichita Lineman," which showcased his appealing tenor voice and skilled guitar work.

Johnny Cash, marching to his own beat, delved into folksongs, protest music, and controversial topics, along the way appealing to everyone from Folsom Prison inmates to young rockers to U.S. presidents. In 1968, he married June Carter, who co-wrote "Ring of Fire" and shared the microphone with Cash on "Jackson" and other hit duets.

Left: Jeannie Seely wore this dress at appearances with Porter Wagoner, c. 1966.

Below left: 1966 Grammy earned by Jeannie Seely for her recording of "Don't Touch Me."

Jeannie Seely

Glen Campbell

Charley Pride overcame racial prejudice to win a huge following and gain tremendous success on the country charts. After Chet Atkins signed the former Negro American League baseball player to RCA in 1965, Pride enjoyed a twenty-year streak of hits that included such classics as "Is Anybody Goin' to San Antone" and "Kiss an Angel Good Mornin'."

In an era of great social upheaval, country music continued to evolve with the times. Its songs reflected changes going on in the culture while maintaining the earthy, honest quality that gave the music its identity.

Left: Charley Pride's 1967 Fender Coronado II hollow-body electric guitar.

Right: Johnny Cash wore this suit while hosting his network TV show.

Charley Pride

June Carter Cash and Johnny Cash

JOHNNY CASH'S 1957 GIBSON SJ-200

The singing cowboy craze of the 1930s didn't just cause the acoustic guitar to balloon in popularity—it ballooned in size as well. The seventeen-inch-wide body of Gibson's SJ-200 ("Super Jumbo") model was designed to project louder volume in the hands of Gene Autry, Ray Whitley, and other cowboy stars. In 1958, Johnny Cash featured this SJ-200—with custom pickguard and his name inlaid in mother-of-pearl on the fingerboard—on the cover of his album *The Fabulous Johnny Cash* and used it to write songs, including "Don't Take Your Guns to Town" and "Five Feet High and Rising."

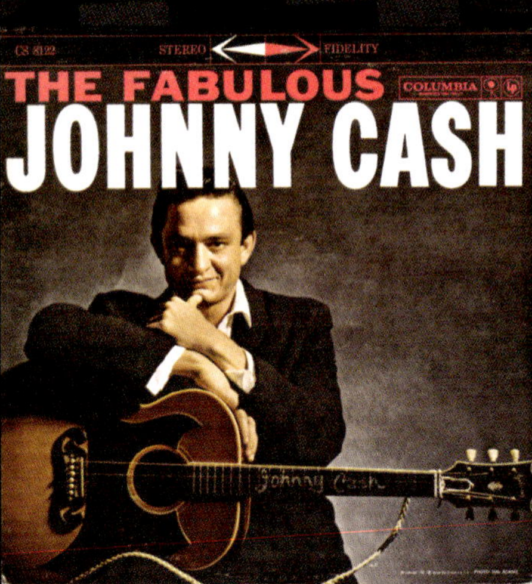

COWBOY JACK CLEMENT'S 1952 GIBSON SJ-200

When the Nashville home studio of record producer, songwriter, and musician Cowboy Jack Clement burned in 2011, he took solace in the fact that his most prized possession was saved from the flames.

"I got my baby," he said, cradling this tobacco sunburst 1952 Gibson SJ-200. "This guitar means more to me than the house."

Clement played his treasured SJ-200—acquired while serving in the Marine Corps—on Johnny Cash recordings such as "Ring of Fire." He also wrote songs for Cash, George Jones, Charley Pride, Porter Wagoner & Dolly Parton, and Waylon Jennings with this instrument.

Kris Kristofferson's U.S. Army uniform shirt.

NASHVILLE SKYLINE

ROCKING BACK TO THE COUNTRY

Before he plunged into folk and revolutionized rock & roll, Bob Dylan first fell in love with country music, tuning into the Grand Ole Opry as a boy and learning the songs of Hank Williams and Hank Snow.

From 1966 to 1969, Dylan recorded three albums in Nashville—*Blonde on Blonde, John Wesley Harding* and *Nashville Skyline*—calling on the city's best country instrumentalists to help bring the "thin . . . wild mercury sound" in his head to life.

Among those musicians was Charlie McCoy, whose brisk, precise playing style on the harmonica shaped the sound of countless classic recordings, from "Delta Dawn" to "He Stopped Loving Her Today." A brilliant multi-instrumentalist, McCoy played bass, guitar, harmonica, and trumpet on Dylan's sessions.

Of course, where Dylan went, many rock musicians followed. The Byrds came to Nashville and recruited country talents such as pedal steel guitarist Lloyd Green for their 1968 album *Sweethearts of the Rodeo*, helping to define the emerging sound of country-rock. Beyond that contribution, Green's sonorous style can be heard on "Elvira," and "D-I-V-O-R-C-E," among more than one hundred chart-topping hits.

Charlie McCoy's bass harmonica.

Bob Dylan

Charlie McCoy

Dylan's work also inspired a new wave of country singer-songwriters, including Kris Kristofferson, who expanded the horizons of country music in the late 1960s with unfettered, emotionally honest songs that spoke to turbulent times. Even as early masterpieces such as "Me and Bobby McGee" and "Sunday Mornin' Comin' Down" found their greatest success in the hands of Janis Joplin and Johnny Cash, the former Army captain soon found the spotlight—not also as just as an artist, but also as one of the leading movie stars of the 1970s.

Kentucky native Tom T. Hall went from penning Jeannie C. Riley's breakout hit "Harper Valley P.T.A." to writing and recording seven of his own chart-toppers—each brimming with absorbing characters, relatable wit, and unvarnished truths—including "Homecoming" and "The Year That Clayton Delaney Died."

Opposite page: Bob Dylan wore this hat during his Rolling Thunder Revue *tour in 1975.*

Below: Lloyd Green's 1967 Sho-Bud Fingertip pedal steel guitar.

George Jones

Tammy Wynette

YOU'RE LOOKING AT COUNTRY

THE OLD WAYS PREVAIL

Southern rock and the Outlaw sounds of Willie Nelson and Waylon Jennings represented country music's tendency to reinvent itself to reflect societal changes. At the same time, several performers held tightly to country's traditional styles.

George Jones, Loretta Lynn, and Tammy Wynette embodied country's fundamental values. Through the 1960s and 1970s, these country stars proudly sang about hard times and bedrock principles. From dirt-poor rural backgrounds, these artists maintained country-proud personas that drew the devotion of fans.

Whether singing honky-tonk or lushly produced ballads, Jones always sounded stone-cold country, with his note-slurring style and his heart-tugging themes. His classic #1 hit "He Stopped Loving Her Today" may soar with orchestrations and harmonies, but it's country to the core.

Right: Tammy Wynette used this Fender Newporter guitar in the late 1960s.

Opposite page: Detail from one of Porter Wagoner's suits made by Nudie's Rodeo Tailors.

Loretta Lynn drew attention with her autobiographical songs, which were as down-home as the Kentucky twang in her instantly identifiable voice. Lynn addressed topics important to women of her time—marriage, family, self-identity, the rise of female empowerment—with spirited narratives that working-class wives could understand.

Tammy Wynette, with her distinct vocal style, sounded fragile yet resilient while addressing the roles of women. Over the course of five marriages—including one to her frequent duet partner Jones—she shared her joys and sorrows in song with compelling emotional honesty.

Left: Porter Wagoner's suit.

Above: Loretta Lynn's dress, which she made herself.

Right: George Jones's boots, made by Nudie's Rodeo Tailors.

Dolly Parton emerged from Appalachia to have a great impact on country music. She first gained notice as the duet partner of successful country singer and TV host Porter Wagoner, then as a singer-songwriter who captured impoverished mountain life in hits such as "Coat of Many Colors." Eventually, she became a world-renowned crossover artist with her popular songs "I Will Always Love You" and "9 to 5," as well as a successful actress, entrepreneur, and philanthropist. Over its twenty-year run on syndicated TV, *The Porter Wagoner Show* influenced public perception of the genre and earned its host a stream of successful singles.

As usual, no matter how far country expanded its sound with new influences, a handful of hard-core traditionalists remained anchored by the genre's sturdiest roots.

Right: Porter Wagoner and Dolly Parton's 1968 CMA Vocal Group of the Year trophy.

Far right: Dolly Parton wore this dress on The Porter Wagoner Show*, c. 1970.*

Loretta Lynn

Porter Wagoner and Dolly Parton

Doug Sahm

Flaco Jiménez

TEXAS MAVERICKS

CREATIVE ESCAPE IN THE LONE STAR STATE

At the start of the 1970s—as Nashville's Outlaws fought for more creative control—the mavericks of Texas were free to dream and expand the possibilities of country music. The capital of Austin was the center of this movement: a town where hippies and rednecks shared the bar counter at venues like Armadillo World Headquarters.

These musicians' influences were all over the map: San Antonio native Doug Sahm, for example, found inspiration both in the psychedelic spirit of the West Coast and the dense musical culture of Texas' Mexican-American population. Flaco

Above: Flaco Jiménez's Hohner Corona II diatonic three-button accordion.

Right: Jerry Jeff Walker's sleeveless denim jacket and jeans.

Jerry Jeff Walker

Asleep at the Wheel

Jiménez was a third-generation accordionist who brought the sounds of conjunto—that's Spanish for "group" or "ensemble"—to listeners far outside its traditional audience.

At Willie Nelson's suggestion, western swing stalwarts Asleep at the Wheel came to Austin from San Francisco in 1973. Within two years, they had a Top Ten country album with their breakthrough *Texas Gold*.

Before each found success on their own, singer-songwriters Jimmie Dale Gilmore, Joe Ely, and Butch Hancock formed the Flatlanders, a talent-brimming outfit with a country sound that blended classic and cosmic elements. There were also freewheeling troubadours like Jerry Jeff Walker—the man who wrote "Mr. Bojangles"—who said he wanted to have his recordings "sound like we were having a grand time at a party thrown for a bunch of our best friends." In the words of Sahm, it was a "Groover's Paradise."

Right: Joe Ely's custom electric guitar, made by Ted Newman Jones.

Below: As a youngster, Doug Sahm played this Fender steel guitar.

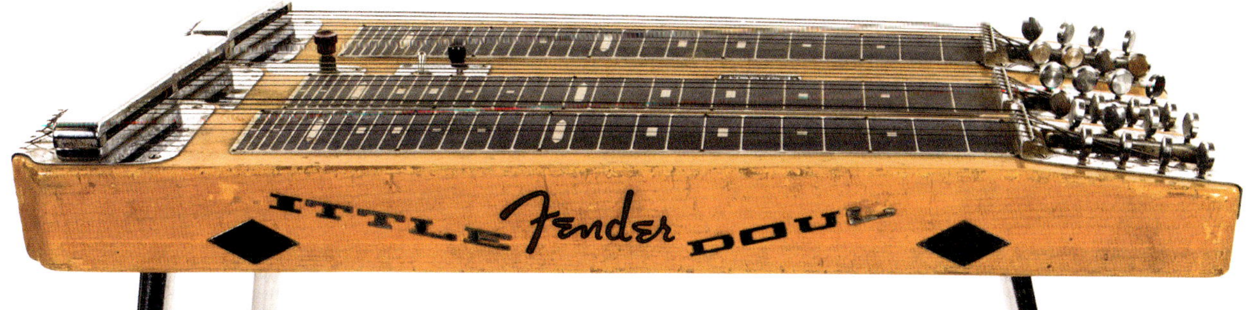

Waylon Jennings

NASHVILLE REBELS

BUCKING THE MUSIC ROW SYSTEM

When Waylon Jennings moved to Nashville in 1965, success came quickly, but artistic independence did not. Over the next decade, Jennings clashed with the powers at RCA Records, demanding the right to choose his own material, recording studio, and musicians. This was a level of creative freedom that was becoming commonplace in rock music, but hadn't yet made its way to Music Row.

Jennings found kindred spirits in Willie Nelson and Bobby Bare, whose careers, like his, flew higher as they gained more control. Soon, they'd also gain a name for their headstrong brand of country—when publicist Hazel Smith dubbed their sound "Outlaw music," the term immediately stuck.

Bandana and sneakers worn by Willie Nelson.

Willie Nelson

Detail from Bobby Bare's hat.

Bare—known for hits such as "Detroit City" and "How I Got to Memphis"—was the first of this group to produce his own albums with 1973's *I Hate Goodbyes / Ride Me Down Easy.* Nelson had left Nashville for his home state of Texas by the time he recorded his landmark album *Red Headed Stranger.* Released in 1975 to critical acclaim and popular success, it launched him to superstar status.

Jennings and Nelson encapsulated this era with the platinum-selling 1976 compilation album *Wanted! The Outlaws,* which also featured recordings from Tompall Glaser and Jennings's wife Jessi Colter. Colter's inclusion on the album reinforced her standing as an artist unwilling to conform

Left: Waylon Jennings wore this Resistol hat and Manuel-designed western shirt.

Right: Willie Nelson gave this hat to Bobby Bare in the early 1970s.

to Nashville's Music Row conventions. Her breakthrough single and signature song, "I'm Not Lisa," was a #1 country and #4 pop hit in 1975.

A bluesy singer, songwriter, and guitarist who grew up in the South, Steve Young wrote "Seven Bridges Road," which became a hit for the Eagles in 1980. Young's personal and artistic nonconformity was an inspiration to Jennings, who recorded his "Lonesome, On'ry and Mean" in 1973.

The successes of the Outlaws expanded country's audience, paved the way for increased creative control, and enhanced commercial opportunities for country recording artists in general.

Right: Jessie Colter wore this suede blouse and skirt on the cover of her album That's the Way a Cowboy Rocks and Rolls.

Jessi Colter

Tompall Glaser

Bobby Bare

THE BANDIT

This 1980 Pontiac Trans Am T-top coupe vas used in the 1980 Hollywood film *Smokey and the Bandit II.* The sequel to *Smokey and the Bandit* (1977) starred Burt Reynolds, Jackie Gleason, Sally Field, erry Reed, and Dom DeLuise. Named fter the character portrayed by Reynolds, "The Bandit" features a five-color firebird lecal on the hood and a 4.9 L turbo ngine. It was later owned by Country Music Hall of Fame member Jerry Reed.

Right: Jerry Reed with Burt Reynolds in the Bandit.

EXIT
TRANS AM
UNIROYAL
STEEL BELTED RADIAL

Boudleaux and Felice Bryant

Hank Cochran

THE SONGWRITER'S CRAFT

THREE CHORDS AND THE TRUTH

Hank Williams made it sound simple when he said, "A song ain't nothin' in the world but a story just wrote with music to it." That may be true, but there's no easy explanation for what makes some of those stories connect with listeners, while others do not.

Songs are the bedrock of country music, but songwriting remains its most compelling mystery. How does a "Cold, Cold Heart" or a "Live Like You Were Dying" get written and sung? Every day, hard-working songwriters rarely seen by country music fans struggle with that very question.

Right: Don Schlitz used this Smith Corona typewriter to write "The Gambler."

Opposite page: Felice and Boudleaux Bryant used this Wollensak reel-to-reel tape recorder to record song ideas and make home demos.

In the 1950s and 1960s, husband and wife team Boudleaux and Felice Bryant found their answer in pairing his melodies with her written verse, then playing the results for artists and producers at their Nashville home over a spaghetti dinner and generous pours of wine. The couple called this approach the "pasta scam," and it led to such hits as "Bye Bye Love" and "Rocky Top."

"I Fall to Pieces" was the first of twenty-nine Top Ten hits written by Hank Cochran. He was a master at translating the pangs of heartbreak into songs such as "Make the World Go Away." Later, a new generation of stars, including George Strait and Keith Whitley, benefitted from his magic.

In 1978, Kenny Rogers was the first artist to release one of Don Schlitz's songs, and that song was "The Gambler," which became the career signature of both musicians. Schlitz instilled many other hit songs with wisdom and eloquence, including "Forever and Ever, Amen" and "When You Say Nothing at All."

Bob McDill approached songwriting like a 9-to-5 job, clocking in every weekday at his office on Music Row. If he hit a snag on one song, he'd move on to another, and another, until quitting time. But for many of today's country songwriters, collaboration is key. Hillary Lindsey's co-written compositions include Carrie Underwood's "Jesus, Take the Wheel," and Little Big Town's "Girl Crush," which she penned with fellow Nashville songwriting greats Lori McKenna and Liz Rose.

Don Schlitz

Bob McDill

Hillary Lindsey

Charlie Daniels

Hank Williams Jr.

Marshall Tucker Band

LONG-HAIRED COUNTRY BOYS

SOUTHERN ROCK GOES COUNTRY

By the close of the 1970s, the boundary between country and rock bands had blurred even more. After the Allman Brothers Band introduced a new form of southern rock—with a biracial lineup that drew on blues, country, folk, jazz, and rock—other young musicians began blending similar influences. Displaying youthful energy and a renewed southern pride, these bands helped the South move beyond the civil rights era toward a period of musical and social integration.

Charlie Daniels and Hank Williams Jr. began scoring hits on the country charts while touting their links to the Marshall Tucker Band and Lynyrd Skynyrd, two southern bands heard on rock radio. A fiddler, guitarist, and songwriter from North Carolina, Daniels first logged rock hits with "Uneasy Rider" and "The South's Gonna Do It Again" before taking "The Devil Went Down to Georgia" to #1 on the country charts in 1979. Daniels continued to record country hits, such as "Drinkin' My Baby Goodbye," through the 1980s.

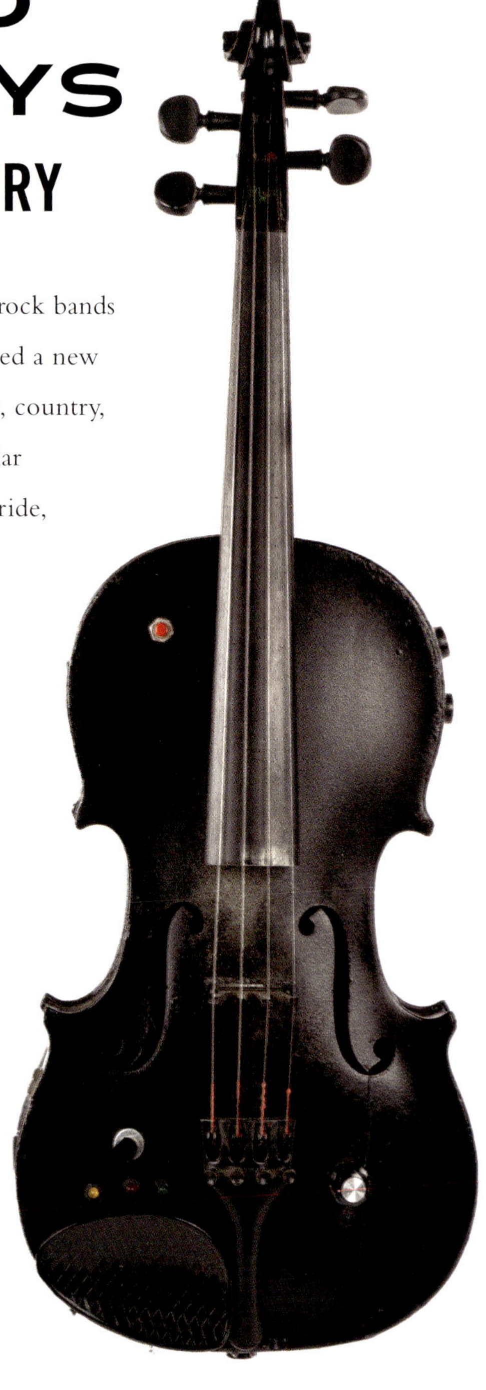

Hank Williams Jr. started out performing his father's songs, but established his own identity by recording with southern rock musicians. After a near-fatal fall down a Montana mountainside, Williams reinvented himself with the country-rock hits "Family Tradition" and "A Country Boy Can Survive." He went on to become the CMA Entertainer of the Year in 1987 and 1988 and the ACM Entertainer of the Year from 1986 to 1988.

By the beginning of the 1980s, a band named for its founders' home state—Alabama—put a polished spin on southern rock. Cousins Randy Owen, Teddy Gentry, and Jeff Cook, along with drummer Mark Herndon, showed how country themes and rock dynamics could be woven into a sound that captivated country audiences. In 1980, they scored their first of twenty-one consecutive #1 country hits with "Tennessee River." After Alabama's success, rock became a significant influence on country artists as generations of musicians grew up listening to both musical forms.

Opposite page: Charlie Daniels used this fiddle when he performed in the 1980 film Urban Cowboy.

Right: Hank Williams Jr. acquired this 1957 Gibson Les Paul from Dickey Betts of the Allman Brothers Band.

Lynyrd Skynyrd

Alabama

Freddy Fender

Charlie Rich

BACK HOME AGAIN

COUNTRY ACHIEVES MAINSTREAM POPULARITY

Ten years after the reign of the Nashville Sound production style, a similar creative philosophy on Music Row earned its own name: "Countrypolitan." Light on traditional country's twang and heavy on lush arrangements and silky vocals, the smooth sound led to pop crossover hits for many country singers, and fostered an open atmosphere where artists from a wider variety of musical backgrounds could find success in the country market.

There was now room for voices like Baldemar Huerta—better known to fans as Freddy Fender—whose soulful rendition of "Before the Next Teardrop Falls" became the first #1 country song to include Spanish lyrics. Charlie Rich found a unique niche in country music with a smooth style that stretched beyond the genre's perceived confines. With the guiding hand of songwriter/producer Billy Sherrill, Rich topped the country charts in 1973 with "Behind Closed Doors" and "The Most Beautiful Girl"—his first of eight #1 country hits.

RJ's Boot Company in Houston made these boots for Charlie Rich, nicknamed "The Silver Fox."

John Denver

Crystal Gayle

John Denver's very first hit (on the pop charts) was "Take Me Home, Country Roads" in 1971, but the country music industry was slow to embrace the folk-inspired singer-songwriter. He found his way in with his 1974 country chart-topper "Back Home Again," and was named the CMA's Entertainer of the Year in 1975.

The youngest sibling of Loretta Lynn, Crystal Gayle (born Brenda Gail Webb) emerged from her sister's shadow by embracing a soothing country-pop sound that favored piano, strings and delicate diction over twang. Working extensively with producer Allen Reynolds, Gayle enjoyed eighteen #1 country hits in the '70s and '80s, including the pop crossover hit "Don't It Make My Brown Eyes Blue."

Right: Freddy Fender wore this rhinestone-embellished outfit in the 1970s.

Far right: John Denver wore this denim and satin tuxedo at the American Music Awards in 1976.

Don Williams

CROSSOVER FEVER

COUNTRY MUSIC TAKES AIM AT THE POP CHARTS

As the 1970s progressed, country music began to reflect the nation's renewed optimism and pop culture's shift toward greater creative freedom for artists. Country stars crossed over into the pop market frequently and exerted a larger presence in the media. From the laid-back, folk-influenced country of Don Williams to the dynamic, soul-inflected pop-country of Ronnie Milsap, the sounds of performers impacting the pop market represented country music's growing diversity.

Don Williams parlayed his gentle croon into a string of chart-toppers such as "Till the Rivers All Run Dry" (1976).

Below: This Stetson hat became an inseparable part of Don Williams.

Right: Ronnie Milsap wore this outfit at the 1978 CMA Awards.

Ronnie Milsap

He became one of the biggest country stars in the world, as popular in England and Europe as in America. In 1974, "Pure Love" became the first of thirty-five #1 hits that kept Ronnie Milsap's up-tempo country-pop sound high in the charts for the next fifteen years.

Sometimes this variety appeared in the work of a single artist. Kenny Rogers and Dottie West, two veterans whose styles changed with the times, achieved across-the-board success, individually and as polished duet partners.

After spending the sixties touring as a teenage instrumentalist touring with Johnny Cash and Patsy Cline, Barbara Mandrell became a star singer—and eventually a household name—with crossover pop hits, an NBC-TV variety series (1980–1982), a best-selling autobiography, and a dynamic Las Vegas stage revue.

Right: Kenny Rogers wore this costume in the 1980 TV movie Kenny Rogers as The Gambler.

Far right: Hollywood designer Bob Mackie created this outfit for Dottie West.

Kenny Rogers

Dottie West

am Bush

MODERN BLUEGRASS

REIMAGINING THE HIGH LONESOME SOUND

In the 1960s and 1970s, a new generation of musicians fell in love with bluegrass—but they weren't afraid to break from its long-held traditions, with shaggy haircuts, electric instrumentation, and the influence of rock, jazz, and music from around the globe. This movement became known as "newgrass," and it massively expanded bluegrass's creative horizons.

Newgrass shares its name with New Grass Revival, an influential group founded by vocalist, mandolinist, and fiddler Sam Bush in 1971. Their work inspired musicians to bring a bolder array of influences and instruments into bluegrass.

Other major players of the era included John Hartford—whose introspective song "Gentle on My Mind" became a country-pop standard—and Vassar Clements, who lent his fiddle stylings to the Nitty Gritty Dirt Band and bridged numerous genres on his album *Hillbilly Jazz*.

John Hartford

Right: Instrument makers Mac Barnes and Kenny Lamb built this custom fiddle for John Hartford.

Far right: John Hartford's Baldwin five-string banjo.

Vassar Clements

Alison Krauss

Del McCoury

That same experimental spirit has remained at the heart of the genre. When Alison Krauss arrived on the scene in the 1980s, lead female vocalists were still a rarity in bluegrass. She became one of the most celebrated singers in any genre, winning more than two-dozen Grammy awards. Longtime bluegrass veteran Del McCoury has eagerly brought his traditional sounds to unlikely spaces, sharing the stage with Phish and other jam bands.

Right: Sam Bush has played this Gibson A-50 mandolin extensively.

Far right: This 1955 Martin D-28 has been used extensively by Del McCoury.

MECHANICAL BULL

This El Toro mechanical bull was used in the hit 1980 movie *Urban Cowboy,* filmed at Gilley's nightclub in Pasadena, Texas. Starring John Travolta and Debra Winger, the film led to a nationwide fascination with country music—so much so that this three-year period of skyrocketing sales and crossover pop hits became known as the "Urban Cowboy" era in country music. Along with songs such as Johnny Lee's "Lookin' for Love" and Anne Murray's "Could I Have This Dance," the film introduced mainstream audiences to mechanical bull-riding, which also would enjoy a spike in national popularity.

Hard hat days and honky-tonk nights.
JOHN TRAVOLTA
URBAN COWBOY
EL TORO
BRONCO SHOP

Ricky Skaggs

The Judds

BACK TO THE FUTURE

NEW TRADITIONALISTS RECLAIM BEDROCK SOUNDS

The 1980 Hollywood film *Urban Cowboy* spotlighted a country dance scene flourishing in spacious nightclubs such as Gilley's in Pasadena, Texas. When the movie became a hit, it inspired a rush on sales of western-style clothing and country albums, some of it leaning toward kitsch. As a result, the term "Urban Cowboy" came to stand for a watered-down version of the country lifestyle.

As the fad ended, a new generation of country artists arrived to re-energize Music Row. Drawing inspiration from the down-to-earth sounds of country music's past, these "new traditionalists," as the media called them, proved that straight-ahead country music could be refashioned to appeal to young music fans.

Right: Naomi Judd's nurse uniform and the tunic Wynonna wore in the video for the Judds' #1 hit "Mama He's Crazy."

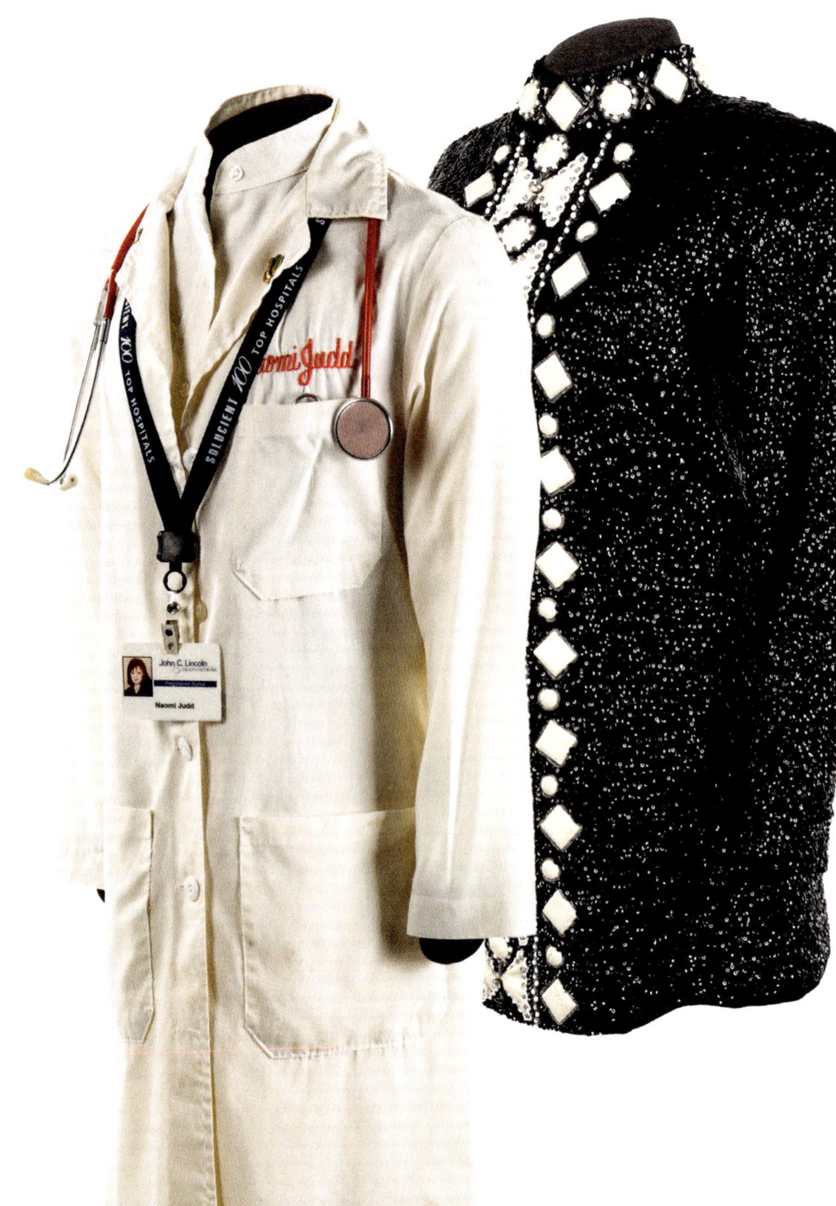

Detail of George Strait's Bud Light team-roping championship buckle.

Ricky Skaggs spent years under the tutelage of bluegrass greats before joining Emmylou Harris's renowned Hot Band. From there, he launched a solo career with an exciting hybrid of bluegrass and contemporary country music that resulted in a string of top hits and awards. Similarly, the Judds used stripped-down, acoustic-based music highlighting Wynonna Judd's husky voice and the sweet harmonies of her mother, Naomi Judd. Combining grassroots and glamour, they became arena headliners until a chronic illness forced Naomi Judd from the road. Wynonna continued as a hit solo artist, while Naomi was an author and TV star until her untimely death in 2022.

George Strait almost singlehandedly revived cowboy fashion and western-swing influences in country music; his movie-star looks, humble stage manner, and steadfast dedication to older musical styles led him to become one of the biggest stars of his era. His enduring success resulted in a record-breaking accumulation of #1 hits, and he continued to sell out concerts nationwide several decades into his career.

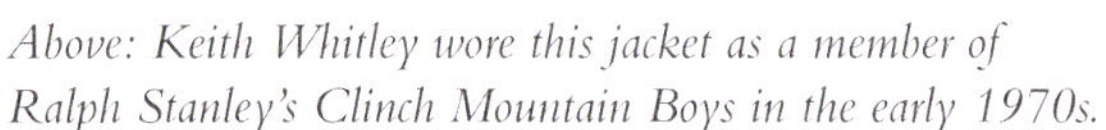

Above: Keith Whitley wore this jacket as a member of Ralph Stanley's Clinch Mountain Boys in the early 1970s.

Right: George Strait's spurs and Resistol cowboy hat.

Randy Travis's debut album, *Storms of Life,* sold three million copies—a rare feat for a country newcomer at the time. Driven by hard-country songs like the #1 hit single "On the Other Hand," it helped reignite radio's interest in the classic country sound of steel guitars and fiddles. It also made a superstar out of Travis, a former juvenile delinquent who matured into a clean-living role model for other young country singers.

Keith Whitley emerged in the mid-1980s as a solo vocalist in the hard-country style of Lefty Frizzell and Merle Haggard. With chart-topping romantic ballads such as "Don't Close Your Eyes" and "When You Say Nothing at All," Whitley revealed a vocal maturity and sensitivity far beyond his years. Only thirty-four when he died in 1989, Whitley left a musical legacy that exerted a profound influence on many younger singers.

Country music would swing back toward pop and rock influences, but the 1980s proved that Nashville could rebound from a drop in popularity and reset its future with a fresh crop of artists who honor the music's roots.

Randy Travis

George Strait

Keith Whitley

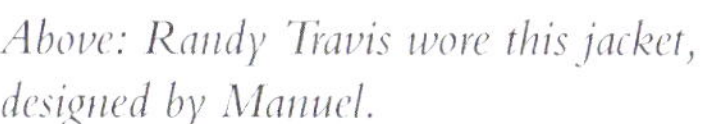

Above: Randy Travis wore this jacket, designed by Manuel.

GUITARS, CADILLACS

COUNTRY MUSIC'S NEW WAVE

The success of Randy Travis, George Strait, the Judds and other new traditionalists proved country fans would welcome performers with fresh twists on classic sounds. Consequently, Nashville's gates opened to a wave of new artists who transformed country music's look and feel.

Dwight Yoakam, a Kentucky-born performer and actor based in Los Angeles, brought a Bakersfield-influenced brashness to his Telecaster-fired country-rock, uniting middle-aged Buck Owens admirers with young rock fans in the process.

Steve Earle swaggered forward with terse, guitar-driven roots-rock that tackled working-class issues and addressed personal demons. He became a sensation with his twanging 1986 album, *Guitar Town*.

Dwight Yoakam

Marty Stuart

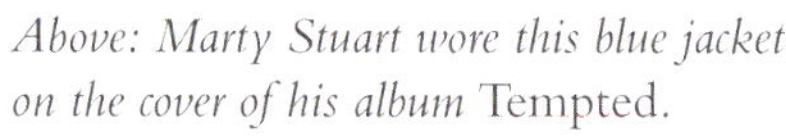

Above: Marty Stuart wore this blue jacket on the cover of his album Tempted.

Right: Dwight Yoakam wore this black jacket and jeans in music videos.

Steve Earle

Nanci Griffith

Marty Stuart learned to play mandolin and guitar as a small boy. He joined Lester Flatt's band at age thirteen and later apprenticed under Doc Watson and Johnny Cash. In the mid-1980s, Stuart began forging a career carrying forward country's traditions, finding success as a recording artist, songwriter, and multimedia emissary for country music.

A self-described "folkabilly" artist, singer-songwriter Nanci Griffith earned acclaim for merging country sounds with folk sensibilities. Both a brilliant songwriter and a masterful interpreter of others' work, she won a Grammy for her 1993 collection of folk music covers, *Other Voices, Other Rooms*.

Together, these and other 1980s artists broadened country music's appeal to fans weaned on the singer-songwriters and folk-rockers of the 1970s, helping set the stage for even greater growth in country music in the 1990s.

Right: Steve Earle played this 1985 Gibson J-100E acoustic-electric model extensively.

Far right: Nanci Griffith wore this skirt and top on the cover of her 1984 album, Once in a Very Blue Moon.

Brooks & Dunn

COUNTRY CLUB

HONKY TONKIN' IN THE MODERN WORLD

In the 1990s, another wave of young, tradition-leaning artists helped keep country music steeped in the sounds of the honky-tonks and Appalachia. These performers were as influenced by George Strait, Emmylou Harris, and Ricky Skaggs as by George Jones, Dolly Parton, and Bill Monroe, and they tempered their love of tradition with a radio-friendly approach that reaped #1 hits, industry awards, and multi-platinum sales. Performers such Brooks & Dunn, Alan Jackson, and Patty Loveless took a humble approach to keeping country music's roots alive.

Emerging in 1991 with their chart-topping debut single, "Brand New Man," Kix Brooks and Ronnie Dunn reigned as country music's top duo for nearly twenty years, thanks to a radio-friendly mix of supercharged roadhouse tunes and smooth ballads, along with a high-energy stage show. They earned twenty #1 hits, several multi-platinum albums, and dozens of industry awards.

Alan Jackson

Alan Jackson's custom guitar, which he played at the CMA Awards in 2001 as he sang "Where Were You (When the World Stopped Turning)."

Detail from Alan Jackson's guitar.

Alan Jackson's 1990 debut album, *Here in the Real World*, displayed his devotion to tradition through songs such as "Wanted" and "Chasin' That Neon Rainbow." His songwriting drew from personal experience, and he delivered clever lyrics as succinct and elequent as those of his heroes Merle Haggard and Hank Williams. Jackson's consistency as a songwriter and recording artist has kept him on the charts well into this century.

Patty Loveless, a coal-miner's daughter like cousin Loretta Lynn, drew on honky-tonk, rockabilly, and mountain harmonies to forge a modern country sound of her own. She won over critics and fans alike while racking up twenty Top Ten hits between 1988 and 1997, including "Timber, I'm Falling in Love" and "Blame It on Your Heart."

Travis Tritt stormed the charts in 1990 while proudly trumpeting his allegiances to hard-country music and bluesy southern rock. Over the course of the decade, he'd release six platinum or multiplatinum albums, and enjoy twenty Top Ten hits, including "I'm Gonna Be Somebody" and "Here's a Quarter (Call Someone Who Cares)."

Left: Patty Loveless wore this jacket and dress when Porter Wagoner invited her to join the Grand Ole Opry cast on June 11, 1988.

Patty Loveless

Travis Tritt

Detail from the back of Travis Tritt's fringed jacket, designed for him in the early 1990s by Barbara Grimes at Gossamer Wings Santa Fe.

POCKET FULL OF GOLD

COUNTRY IN THE AGE OF PLENTY

In September 1991, Garth Brooks became the first country music artist to have an album debut at the top spot on *Billboard* magazine's chart of best-selling albums in the nation, spanning all genres. The feat coincided with the arrival of a new technology, SoundScan, that tallied sales totals at the cash register rather than by reports from retailers. Removing bias from the procedure, it became apparent that country albums were selling in greater numbers than previously reported—and that Garth Brooks was the hottest recording artist in America.

Brooks's enormous sales power, and that of veterans such as George Strait and newcomers such as Alan Jackson and Vince Gill, astonished the media and the music industry. Simultaneously, country radio ruled the airwaves. Country music officially had entered the American entertainment mainstream.

Right: Garth Brooks wore this Stetson on the cover of his 1989 self-titled debut album. He wore this Panhandle Slim western shirt on the cover of his second album, No Fences *(1990).*

Buoyed by this success, Nashville ushered in talented young men in cowboy hats and western attire—inspiring the term "hat act." The best of these singers distinguished themselves, usually by combining traditional and contemporary sounds in distinctive ways.

Garth Brooks cited "my two Georges"—Jones and Strait—as his influences, but also acknowledged a debt to singer-songwriters James Taylor and Dan Fogelberg, and arena-rock acts KISS and Kansas. The results balanced acoustic balladry with barroom country music and classic rock, all of which Brooks helped sell with a dynamic stage show.

Vince Gill blended bluegrass and country music into a sensitive yet stirring style that highlighted his beautiful tenor voice and his dazzling musicality on guitar. Already an established star, Reba McEntire built an entertainment empire in the 1990s, embarking on a successful film and television acting career while continuing to top the country charts. Other early '90s successes included Tim McGraw, who caught fire with clever sing-alongs and touching ballads, but soon expanded his sound with rock influences that brought greater sophistication to his messages.

By the new century, country artists regularly topped the *Billboard* all-genre album charts and frequently appeared on television and in films—maintaining the strides made during country's 1990s explosion.

Below: Vince Gill's shoes, which he wore hosting the CMA Awards (1992–2003).

Right: Barbie Dolls of Tim McGraw and Faith Hill.

Reba McEntire

Tim McGraw

Faith Hill

Shania Twain

Trisha Yearwood

LET'S GO GIRLS

FEMALE ARTISTS TAKE THE WHEEL

"Let's go, girls."

Those three words at the start of Shania Twain's 1999 hit single "Man! I Feel Like a Woman" played like a proclamation for the country music industry in the 1990s, as female voices became equally important to the genre's success, acclaim, and visibility.

Standing on the shoulders of groundbreaking artists Kitty Wells, Tammy Wynette, Loretta Lynn, and Dolly Parton, female country singers in the 1990s advanced themes that emphasized confidence, pride, and self-determination. Whether rejecting bad men or celebrating love's joys, women felt empowered to boldly share their perspectives.

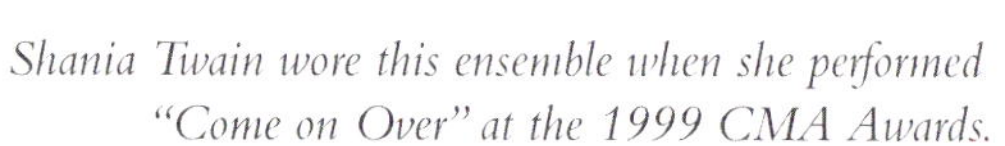

Shania Twain wore this ensemble when she performed "Come on Over" at the 1999 CMA Awards.

Opposite: Detail from Trisha Yearwood's boots.

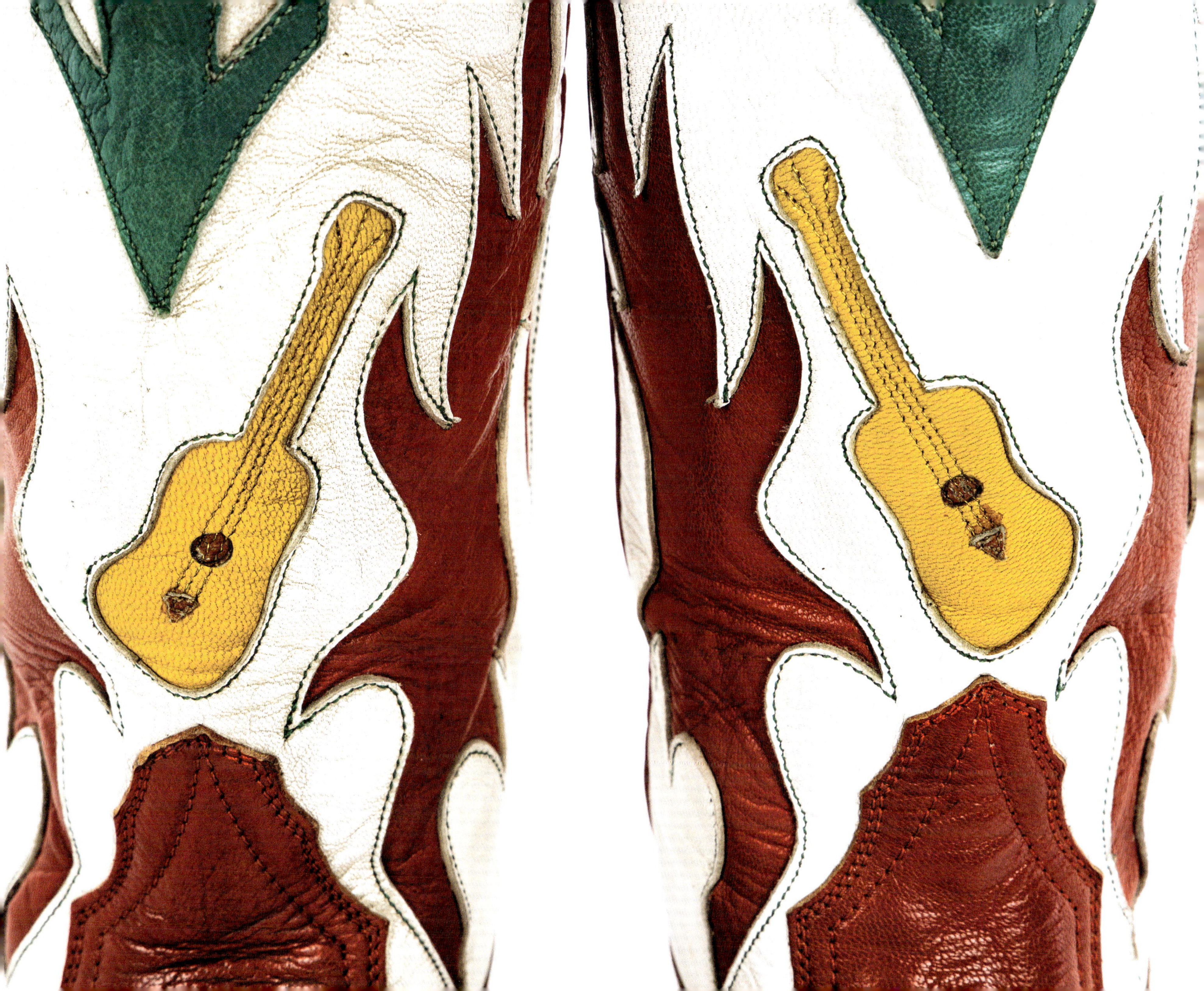

Shania Twain and Robert John "Mutt" Lange—her producer, co-writer, and then-husband—together created an influential pop-country sound that brought Twain unprecedented commercial success and signaled a new era for female country singers. Her 1997 album *Come On Over* sold more than twenty million copies, making it the best-selling album in history by a female artist, in any genre.

Trisha Yearwood's powerful voice lent force to lyrics that expressed a confident female perspective. Her first single, "She's in Love with the Boy," found the subject going against her father's wishes while following her heart, and the exuberant song rocketed to #1. Her debut album sold a million copies in its first year.

Martina McBride purposefully set out to record what she called "strong-woman material" after her tradition-based debut album didn't sell well. The change lifted her career. Her 1993 album *The Way That I Am* featured a song about rising up against domestic abuse ("Independence Day") and a celebration of self-acceptance ("My Baby Loves Me"). McBride's muscular voice became an enduring fixture on country radio.

Left: Martina McBride's outfit when she was pregnant and performing at the 1994 CMA Awards.

Right: Trisha Yearwood's custom boots.

As assertive female voices prospered in rock and pop in the late 1990s, Nashville found its winning equivalent in the Dixie Chicks. The trio's first two major-label albums both sold more than ten million copies, featuring hits such as "Wide Open Spaces" and "Goodbye Earl." After vocalist Natalie Maines criticized the US-led invasion of Iraq in 2003, the group immediately fell out of favor in the country market, but still won the Grammy for Album of the Year for 2006's *Taking the Long Way*.

The Chicks' outfits for the Grammy Awards in 1999.

Martina McBride

The Chicks

JOHN PRINE'S JUKEBOX

Singer-songwriter John Prine received this 1942 Wurlitzer jukebox as a gift from friend and fellow singer-songwriter Steve Goodman, who wanted to thank him for co-writing his first country hit—and refusing to take credit. During a late night in the summer of 1971, Prine returned to the New York City hotel room he was sharing with Goodman to find him working on a new song.

"Well, it was all that I could do to keep from crying," the lyrics began. "Sometimes it seems so useless to remain."

Prine, fresh from the bars in Greenwich Village, wanted to lighten the mood. He helped Goodman turn the song into "You Never Even Called Me by My Name," a gentle lampooning of country music cliches.

But when Goodman recorded it for his debut album, Prine didn't want credit or compensation for a song he thought might be seen as an insult to the genre. He didn't change his mind in 1975, when a version by David Allan Coe rose to #8 on *Billboard*'s Hot Country Singles chart and earned Goodman substantial royalties.

To show his gratitude, Goodman used part of his royalties to buy his friend a jukebox, an old-fashioned, automated record-playing machine once popular in bars and restaurants. Prine made this Wurlitzer his own, filling it with classic and obscure country, pop, and R&B singles, even several Christmas carols. He told *Rolling Stone* the jukebox reminded him of his father, an Illinois factory worker who would bring John and his brothers along to local honky-tonks, where they often heard such songs.

Inset above: Steve Goodman (left) and John Prine.

37
WURLITZER

Jim Lauderdale

Buddy Miller

AMERICANA MUSIC

A HOME FOR THE OUTSIDERS

Over the course of the 1990s, American roots musicians playing the time-honored sounds of country, folk, blues, and soul found a home in a new musical category: "Americana." Many of these artists had no qualms about blending those styles into something distinctly authentic and undeniably American. The wide-ranging genre gained its first record chart in January 1995, when *The Gavin Report* trade magazine launched its Americana chart to track radio airplay of roots music. The genre soon became a haven for young artists with old souls, mainstream country outcasts, and esteemed veterans to spread their wings.

Jim Lauderdale's freewheeling, eclectic blend of country, bluegrass, and rock made him a quintessential Americana artist well before the term gained prominence. While garnering critical praise, the singer and guitarist churned through several major-label record deals in the 1990s, but he found steady success as a songwriter, writing "You Don't Seem to Miss Me" for Patty Loveless and George Jones, and having a hand in more than dozen songs cut by George Strait.

Jim Lauderdale wore this outfit in the 2019 music video for his song "Listen."

Detail of Buddy Miller's Wandre Soloist electric guitar.

As a recording artist, guitar player, songwriter, producer, and bandleader, Buddy Miller has worked with a host of influential music-makers, including Robert Plant, Alison Krauss, and Emmylou Harris—as well as singer-songwriter Julie Miller, his wife of more than forty years. Their first collaborative project, *Buddy & Julie Miller*, was named Album of the Year at the inaugural Americana Music Honors & Awards in 2002.

A MacArthur Genius grant recipient and Pulitzer Prize winner, Rhiannon Giddens has dedicated her career to shining a light on the origins of American music. In 2005, she co-founded the Grammy-winning group Carolina Chocolate Drops, who performed in the centuries-old tradition

Far left: Buddy Miller purchased this Wandre Soloist electric guitar for $50 in 1976. It became one of his mainstay guitars for live and studio work.

Left: Owned and played by Rhiannon Giddens, this instrument is a reproduction of a banjo built in 1858 by Levi Brown in Baltimore, Maryland.

Rhiannon Giddens

of Black stringbands. As she embarked on a solo career, she also founded the supergroup Our Native Daughters, whose work raised awareness of country music's Black roots. Her banjo playing can be heard on Beyoncé's 2024 chart-topper "Texas Hold 'Em."

Gillian Welch and David Rawlings's spare and intimate acoustic-based songs hearkened back to the mountain music of Depression-era Appalachia, helping to rekindle interest in traditional country sounds. After contributing to the landmark *O Brother, Where Art Thou* soundtrack, the pair made massive songwriting strides on their 2001 masterwork *Time (The Revelator)*, incorporating a more modern sensibility and elements of contemporary playing into their traditional sound.

Right: David Rawlings has used this 1934 Epiphone Masterbilt Olympic archtop guitar in the recording studio and at live performances.

Far right: Rawlings's musical partner, Gillian Welch, wore this 1930s vintage floral-print dress on the front cover of her 2001 album, Time (The Revelator).

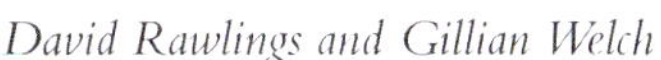

David Rawlings and Gillian Welch

A select few musical instruments have become country music icons. The music fashioned on them helped shape American culture.

LESTER FLATT'S MARTIN D-28

Lester Flatt helped popularize and shape bluegrass music with his warm, distinctive vocals and his solid rhythm guitar work as a partner with Earl Scruggs in Flatt & Scruggs and, before that, as a member of Bill Monroe's Blue Grass Boys. Flatt's instrumental style is closely associated with this 1950 Martin D-28, which he purchased in 1956 from a West Virginia pawnshop. He went on to use the instrument on most Flatt & Scruggs recordings and performances.

Former Flatt sideman Marty Stuart described the Martin, with its rich tone, as "possibly one of the greatest rhythm instruments ever made." Stuart donated the instrument to the Country Music Hall of Fame and Museum, and prior to that he used the guitar himself.

These treasures are currently displayed as part of the museum's collection—and serve as enduring symbols of the power of music.

EARL SCRUGGS'S GIBSON RB-GRANADA MASTERTONE

With typical humility, Earl Scruggs described his beloved Gibson banjo as "just an old hand-me-down." But the master of the five-string banjo used the instrument, manufactured in 1930, to further develop his three-finger picking style and elevate bluegrass as a genre that highlighted superb musicianship.

Scruggs got the Granada in a trade with fellow bluegrass legend Don Reno in the late 1940s. The Flatt & Scruggs 1949 classic "Foggy Mountain Breakdown," written by Scruggs, showcased his astounding speed and clarity on the instrument.

Scruggs used the Granada as his primary instrument on the road and in the studio with Flatt & Scruggs and later with the Earl Scruggs Revue. He continued to play the instrument until his death in 2012.

Detail of Brad Paisley's first guitar, a Sears Silvertone Model 1421.

CONNECTED LIKE NEVER BEFORE

COUNTRY MUSIC IN THE DIGITAL AGE

The new millennium brought turmoil and change, as the music industry struggled with challenges presented by the internet. Digital downloading reduced CD sales, and major labels signed fewer artists. Corporate consolidation tightened radio playlists, increasing competition for hit singles.

Nonetheless, country music adapted to new technology, as it always has. Artists drew from hard rock, hip-hop, and island rhythms to reach younger audiences. The internet, satellite radio, and TV provided new means to deliver country music. Web pages and social media enabled artists to communicate directly with fans.

Successful performers such as Dierks Bentley, Brad Paisley, and Keith Urban also forged careers in tried-and-true ways: they concentrated on constant touring with exciting live shows while creating distinctive identities through song choices and presenting themselves to fans in singular ways.

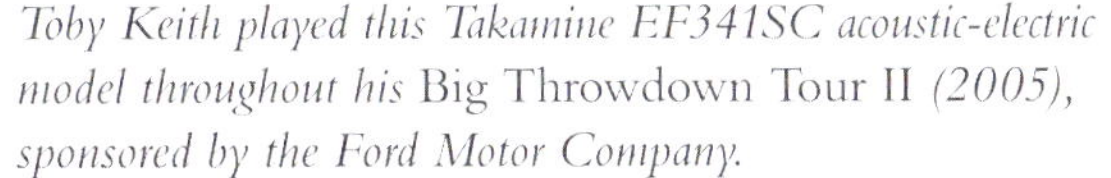

Toby Keith played this Takamine EF341SC acoustic-electric model throughout his Big Throwdown Tour II *(2005), sponsored by the Ford Motor Company.*

Dierks Bentley

Brad Paisley

Keith Urban

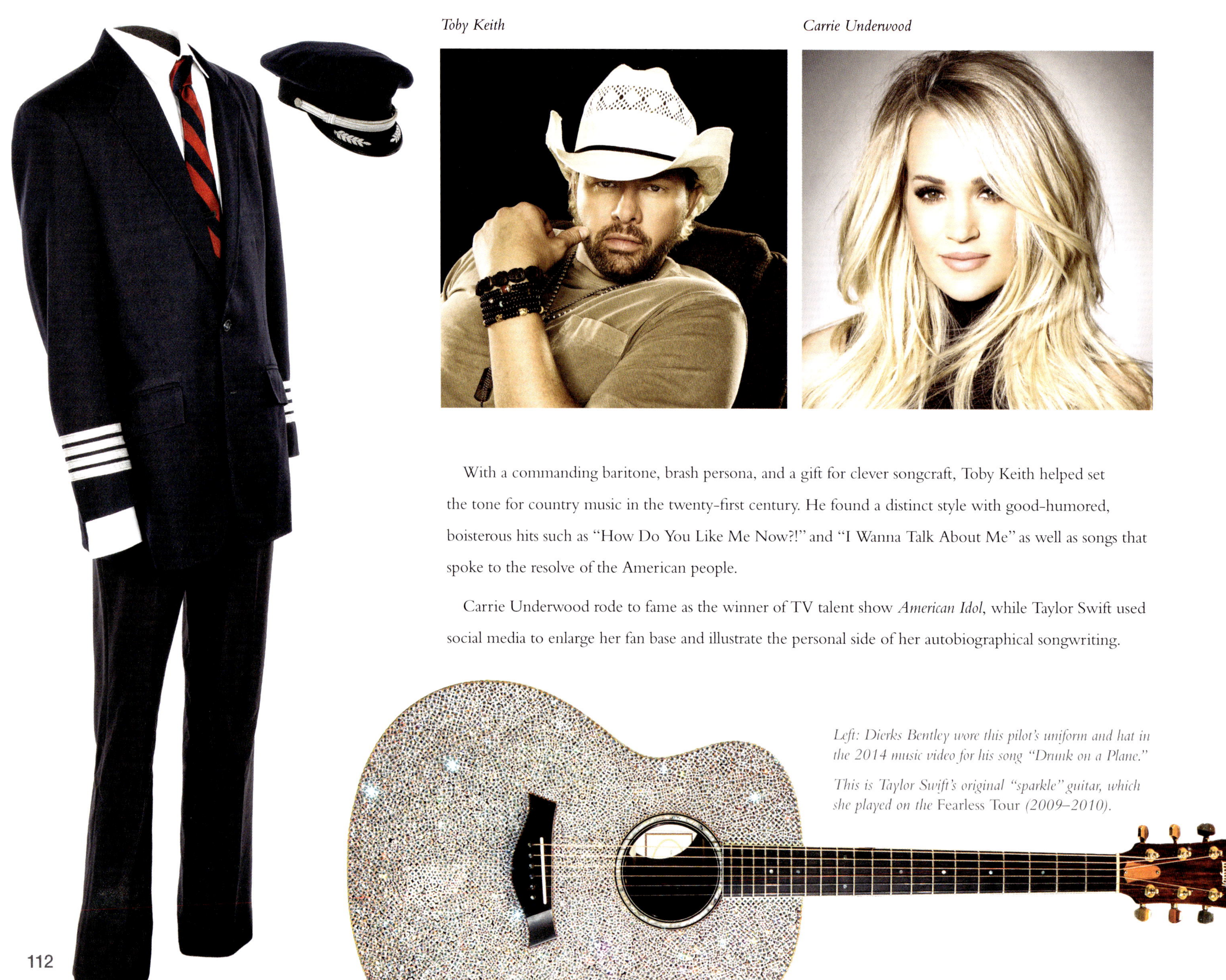

Toby Keith

Carrie Underwood

With a commanding baritone, brash persona, and a gift for clever songcraft, Toby Keith helped set the tone for country music in the twenty-first century. He found a distinct style with good-humored, boisterous hits such as "How Do You Like Me Now?!" and "I Wanna Talk About Me" as well as songs that spoke to the resolve of the American people.

Carrie Underwood rode to fame as the winner of TV talent show *American Idol*, while Taylor Swift used social media to enlarge her fan base and illustrate the personal side of her autobiographical songwriting.

Left: Dierks Bentley wore this pilot's uniform and hat in the 2014 music video for his song "Drunk on a Plane."

This is Taylor Swift's original "sparkle" guitar, which she played on the Fearless Tour *(2009–2010).*

Taylor Swift

Blake Shelton

Combining a liberated perspective with girl-next-door appeal, Faith Hill embraced a pop-influenced sound at the turn of the century, with three of her albums topping *Billboard's* country and all-genre album charts.

A confident baritone, rugged good looks, and penchant for wisecracks all added up to Blake Shelton becoming one of country music's brightest stars—especially once he became a coach on NBC-TV's *The Voice* in 2011. Shelton was named CMA Entertainer of the Year in 2012 and has scored more than thirty Top Ten country hits in his career.

As these artists proved, country music continued to remain relevant, even in an era of rapid cultural and technological change.

Above: Blake Shelton wore this Scully western shirt in the 2004 music video for his #1 hit "Some Beach."

Right: Keith Urban wore this Converse graphic T-shirt and these jeans, when he played Nashville's Bridgestone Arena, May 10, 2013.

Florida Georgia Line

Luke Bryan

Jason Aldean

MIX IT UP STRONG

COUNTRY POWERS UP WITH NEW SOUNDS

With their 2012 debut single "Cruise," country duo Florida Georgia Line ushered in, and soon came to symbolize, the reign of "bro-country" in the 2010s. The party hearty, male-dominated sound let the good times roll, a popular soundtrack for an endless summer of tailgate parties, bonfires, and other simple pleasures.

In this landscape, Luke Bryan emerged as one of the decade's defining male country voices with party anthems including "Country Girl (Shake It for Me)," as well as emotionally resonant songs of loss and contemplation. He was named the CMA's Entertainer of the Year in 2014 and 2015.

Left: Jason Aldean wore this straw cowboy hat in his 2009 music video for "The Truth," a #1 country hit.

Right: Luke Bryan wore this T-shirt with the logo of his high school team, the Lee County Trojans, and these jeans when he performed at Gillette Stadium in Foxborough, Massachusetts, August 10, 2014.

Opposite page: Detail from Kacey Musgraves's costume.

Jason Aldean's blend of hard-rock crunch and hip-hop rhythms—exemplified in his 2011 smash "Dirt Road Anthem"—brought him to the top of the country music charts. He was named the Entertainer of the Year by the Academy of Country Music three years in a row (2016–2018).

At the same time, rootsy traditionalists drew from the time-tested sounds of folk, classic country, and southern soul to bring a broader audience to the genre. Chris Stapleton became an unlikely superstar with his 2015 album *Traveller*, proving that an old-school musical approach had just as much commercial potential as country's newest sound. Darius Rucker enjoyed the biggest hit of his career with "Wagon Wheel," a rollicking folk-country tune originally recorded by contemporary stringband Old Crow Medicine Show.

Above: Kacey Musgraves wore this dress when she performed "Follow Your Arrow" at the Grammy Awards in 2014.

Right: Chris Stapleton owned and used this rare 1959 Martin D-18E, which was the Martin Guitar Company's earliest acoustic-electric model.

Kacey Musgraves married vintage country style with a progressive outlook, earning critical praise and the Grammy for Album of the Year in 2019. With powerful, soul-baring songs such as "Cover Me Up," the Alabama-bred Jason Isbell assumed a place among the most admired singer-songwriters of his generation.

Along with the newcomers, many established country stars found success in this new, no-frills landscape. Long a critical favorite, Miranda Lambert reached new heights of acclaim with 2016's sprawling and sonically rugged *The Weight of These Wings*.

Eric Church called his own creative shots and flaunted his outsider status, while forging a lasting bond with his fans—dubbed "The Church Choir." In 2015, Church sent his fan club members the first copies of his album *Mr. Misunderstood* before announcing its release to the public.

Jason Isbell

Miranda Lambert

Eric Church

Right: Jason Isbell's First Act Custom Delgada LS electric guitar.

Far right: Eric Church wore this two-tone leather jacket, shirt, and jeans on the cover of his 2014 album, The Outsiders.

Kelsea Ballerini

Mickey Guyton

Ashley McBryde

JUST A CLICK AWAY

SOCIAL MEDIA CHANGES THE GAME

As country music approached the 2020s, the digital realm wasn't just a growing sector of the music industry—it was turning into the playing field, and the place where much of the business of music was conducted. The ubiquity of social media led to many artists first building their own audience before attracting record label interest—and it became a paramount way for established acts to maintain a strong connection with their fans.

Kane Brown was one of the first country stars to emerge via social media, bringing a fresh, smooth, and versatile musical style to the genre in the mid-2010s. Meanwhile, the dominance of streaming, and its effect on chart positions, changed the way country music was written, recorded, and packaged. Morgan Wallen's 2021 second effort *Dangerous: The Double Album* spent ten consecutive weeks atop the all-genre albums chart, with hits "7 Summers" and "Wasted on You" among its thirty tracks.

A new generation of assertive, distinct female voices rose to prominence. Kelsea Ballerini, Mickey Guyton, Ashley McBryde, and Carly Pearce made powerful connections with audiences through songs of perseverance in the face of heartbreak and social injustice.

Mickey Guyton wore this silk satin chiffon gown on the cover of her debut album, Remember Her Name *(2021).*

Detail from the back of Lil Nas X's Union Western suit.

With the release of her 2022 album *Bell Bottom Country,* Lainey Wilson became the genre's first new female superstar of the decade. Its success led to her being voted the CMA's 2023 Entertainer of the Year—making her the first woman to win the award in twelve years.

There was room for outliers, as well. With blistering guitar picking and a deep reverence for roots music traditions, Billy Strings carved out a career unlike anything the bluegrass world had seen before, earning a fervent, dedicated following in the same mold as rock's "jam bands."

Blending contemporary rap with western twang and cowboy imagery, "Old Town Road" catapulted nineteen-year-old Montero Hill (a.k.a. Lil Nas X) to superstardom in 2019, and became the

Left: Lainey Wilson wore this silk halter top and pants in her role as Abby in the TV series Yellowstone.

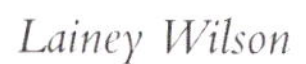

Lainey Wilson

Carly Pearce

longest-running #1 hit in the history of *Billboard*'s Hot 100 chart. Its success foreshadowed an era of high-profile country crossovers from pop stars such as Beyoncé and Post Malone.

As the popular works of these artists show, country music continues to remain relevant, even in an era of rapid cultural and technological change. Will the circle be unbroken, as the famous song asks. Country music's continuing popularity says it will.

Right: Billy Strings wore this poncho and these bleached denim jeans on the opening night of his Meet Me at the Drive-In Tour, *September 11, 2020.*

Far right: Lil Nas X wore this custom Union Western suit in the 2019 music video for "Old Town Road (Remix).

Billy Strings

Lil Nas X

EYEBROW
KELSEY WALDON
NAT MYERS

Tyler Childers

Molly Tuttle

AMERICAN CURRENTS

HISTORY IN THE MAKING

As a popular art form, country music evolves constantly. Like earlier generations, the artists of today create hits that supercharge the music with new influences and ideas. They continue a line that stretches back decades, in which performers combine contemporary and traditional sounds. Those who do so with freshness and ingenuity move the music forward and become celebrated, just as their heroes were before them.

The music's ongoing evolution plays a major role in maintaining its popularity. A few generations ago, the national media rarely featured country music performers. Today, country artists appear on network TV programs, on magazine covers, and on syndicated talk shows, and they generate excitement on social media. More country stars sell out stadium concerts than do those in other genres. The music of the people, country, is now a daily part of the lives of millions.

Right: Shelby Lynne played this 1966 Fender Mustang bass at recording sessions for her 2024 album, Consequences of the Crown.

Opposite page: Kelsey Waldon admires her exhibit in American Currents.

Megan Moroney

Even as country music's sonic palette expands, its songs remain rooted in the sounds of earlier eras. Young artists draw from those who came before them and produce music that branches out from established roots. In time, today's hits will inspire a new generation of young creators; new branches will develop, sprouting more ideas and more growth.

This unending cycle of song has been in motion throughout country music history. Each time a voice carries a melody or a pick strikes a string, an echo of the innovations of pioneers such as Mother Maybelle Carter, Bill Monroe, and Jimmie Rodgers resonates through the ages.

Jelly Roll

Left: Post Malone wore this vintage Nudie jacket when he appeared in the 2024 video for Dwight Yoakam's "I Don't Know How to Say Goodbye (Bang Bang Boom Boom)."

Zach Bryan

Today's successful artists speak often of those who influenced them. Luke Combs, who scored his first major hits in 2017, grew up in western North Carolina and attended Appalachian State University, just as Eric Church had done a decade earlier. Combs saw Church as a role model, feeding off Church's distinctive songwriting and bold attitude in pursuit of his own career. Church himself had drawn similar inspiration from artists such as Hank Williams Jr.—and Church now proudly owns a necklace given to him by Williams. One generation fuels the creativity of the next group of ambitious hopefuls, and country music's lineage keeps extending into the future.

The Country Music Hall of Fame and Museum collects, preserves, and exhibits the music of today for the same reason it gathers and gives context to the artistry and artifacts of the past. Today's music becomes tomorrow's history, and it deserves to be treated with the same attention and care.

Right: Amythyst Kiah wore this leopard-print jacket and pants, and this tuxedo shirt when she made her Grand Ole Opry debut, June 29, 2021.

The War and Treaty

382

THE SOURCES OF COUNTRY MUSIC

BY THOMAS HART BENTON

Renowned American painter Thomas Hart Benton capped his career with *The Sources of Country Music,* a remarkable mural expressing his love for many forms of American traditional music, all of which influenced the commercial art form known as country music.

Commissioned by the Country Music Hall of Fame and Museum, the mural received its last touches from the eighty-five-year-old painter at his Kansas City carriage-house studio, on January 18, 1975, the day before he died.

The sketches and dioramas Benton created during the making of his artwork are now part of the archives of the Country Music Hall of Fame and Museum.

COUNTRY MUSIC HALL OF FAME

Election to the Country Music Hall of Fame is country music's highest honor. The Country Music Association created the Hall of Fame in 1961 and continues to select new members each year.

The museum's Hall of Fame Rotunda is a space of dignity and beauty that recognizes all members, with no individual given special precedence over another. The Hall of Fame plaques are positioned randomly on the walls to ensure that everyone has a place of equal importance. The Rotunda's peaceful atmosphere inspires reverence for the deepest roots of the music and for the significant figures in the music's history.

L THE CIRCLE BE UNBROK

Singing "Will the Circle Be Unbroken" at the conclusion of the June 2008 Medallion Ceremony.
Left to right: Ray Walker of the Jordanaires; Little Jimmy Dickens; Reba McEntire (partially obscured); Gordon Stoker of the Jordanaires; Sonny James; Phil Balsley of the Statler Brothers; Vince Gill; Jo Walker-Meador (obscured); Tom T. Hall; Brenda Lee; Don Reid of the Statler Brothers; Ralph Emery; Earl Scruggs; Jim Foglesong; Jimmy Fortune of the Statler Brothers.

THE COUNTRY MUSIC HALL OF FAME

COUNTRY MUSIC'S GREATEST HONOR

1961 (YEAR INDUCTED)

JIMMIE RODGERS

b. September 8, 1897; d. May 26, 1933 ▪ Birthplace: Meridian, Mississippi

His many nicknames—the Father of Country Music, the Singing Brakeman, America's Blue Yodeler—suggest not only Jimmie Rodgers's stature in American music, but also his artistic range. His highly original music—songs encompassing blues, early jazz and swing, sentimental tunes, traditional music, work chants, and yodeling—influenced generations of singers and songwriters.

FRED ROSE

b. August 24, 1897; d. December 1, 1954 ▪ Evansville, Indiana

Drawing on a background in songwriting and performing in Chicago, New York, and Los Angeles, Fred Rose helped build the Nashville music industry. A partner in Acuff-Rose Publications, he signed Hank Williams to a songwriting contract and produced his recordings, and composed many pop, western, and country classics himself, including "Deed I Do," "Roly Poly," and "Blue Eyes Crying in the Rain."

HANK WILLIAMS

b. September 17, 1923; d. January 1, 1953 ▪ Mount Olive, Alabama

Hank Williams, one of country music's most towering musical figures, only recorded for six years before his early death. But the power of his work set the stage for contemporary country songcraft, and he riveted audiences with his voice and charisma onstage, on recordings, on radio, and on television.

1962

ROY ACUFF

b. September 15, 1903; d. November 23, 1992 ▪ Maynardville, Tennessee

Roy Acuff's popular updating of rural stringband music made him one of the first national stars of the Grand Ole Opry, and he remained a pillar of the famous Nashville institution a half-century later at his death. Known as the King of Country Music, he cofounded Acuff-Rose Publications, an important cornerstone of the Nashville music industry.

1963

(No Inductions)

1964

TEX RITTER

b. January 12, 1905; d. January 2, 1974 ▪ Panola County, Texas

Tex Ritter came to western music honestly, immersing himself in cowboy songs while growing up in Texas. His deep voice and theatrical sensibility led him to star in Broadway musicals and Hollywood films. He later helped solidify Nashville's reputation by becoming a Grand Ole Opry star, radio host, and CMA president.

1965

ERNEST TUBB

b. February 9, 1914; d. September 6, 1984 ▪ near Crisp, Texas

With his distinctive baritone voice and laconic style, Ernest Tubb became one of country music's first honky-tonk stars. He helped usher in the electric guitar as a primary country instrument, and his focus on good musicianship, non-stop touring, and helping up-and-coming artists made him a beloved and influential figure.

Cindy Walker at the 1997 CMA Awards.

1966

EDDY ARNOLD

b. May 15, 1918; d. May 8, 2008 ▪ Henderson, Tennessee

Eddy Arnold, with his smooth voice and refined manner, personified country music's adaptation to a modern, more urban world and its transition from folk-based sounds to pop-influenced ones. By scoring Top Ten hits from the 1940s to 1980, he enjoyed one of American music's most enduring music careers.

JIM DENNY

b. February 28, 1911; d. August 27, 1963 ▪ Buffalo Valley, Tennessee

Longtime manager of the Grand Ole Opry Artists Service, Jim Denny eventually left Nashville's WSM to become one of the most successful talent agents and song publishers in country music history. He formed Cedarwood Publishing Company in 1953 with Webb Pierce, and he later owned several radio stations.

GEORGE D. HAY

b. November 9, 1895; d. May 8, 1968 ▪ Attica, Indiana

Founder of WSM's Grand Ole Opry, George D. Hay played a vital role in commercializing country music and helping form its rural image in its early years. Known as "the Solemn Old Judge," he named the Opry in an impromptu on-air statement in 1927 and long served as its chief announcer, publicist, and spokesman.

UNCLE DAVE MACON

b. October 7, 1870; d. March 22, 1952 ▪ Smart Station, Tennessee

An early star of the Grand Ole Opry, Uncle Dave Macon ranks among the most colorful figures in American entertainment history. A skilled banjo player, strong singer, and mirthful comedian, the master showman bridged the vaudeville tradition of the nineteenth century and the commercial music that followed the advent of radio and phonographs.

1967

RED FOLEY

b. June 17, 1910; d. September 19, 1968 ▪ Blue Lick, Kentucky

Singer Red Foley helped spread country music's popularity through recordings, concerts, and high-profile roles on radio and television programs in Chicago, Cincinnati, Nashville, and Springfield, Missouri. He created classic hits with sentimental songs ("Old Shep"), boogie tunes ("Tennessee Saturday Night"), pop-swing ("Chattanoogie Shoe Shine Boy"), and gospel ("Peace in the Valley").

J. L. FRANK

b. April 15, 1900; d. May 4, 1952 ▪ Limestone County, Alabama

Joseph Lee "J. L." Frank became the first major country music promoter and manager in Nashville. After working in Chicago booking Gene Autry, Frank eventually relocated to Nashville and promoted shows starring Roy Acuff, Eddy Arnold, Pee Wee King, Minnie Pearl, Ernest Tubb, and other Grand Ole Opry stars.

JIM REEVES

b. August 20, 1923; d. July 31, 1964 ▪ Panola County, Texas

The velvet-smooth baritone of Jim Reeves made him one of country music's most distinctive singers and one of the biggest crossover stars of his era. After enjoying hits in Louisiana, Reeves moved to Nashville and joined the Grand Ole Opry. His intimate vocals complemented the lush, sophisticated production style known as the Nashville Sound.

STEVE SHOLES

b. February 12, 1911; d. April 22, 1968 ▪ Washington, D.C.

Record executive and producer Steve Sholes helped shepherd country music's growth and publicize its cultural importance in the years following World War II. He signed Eddy Arnold, Chet Atkins, the Browns, Pee Wee King, Elvis Presley, Jim Reeves, and Hank Snow to RCA Records, and he gave Atkins his start as a leading Nashville producer and RCA executive.

1968

BOB WILLS

b. March 6, 1905; d. May 13, 1975 ▪ Kosse, Texas

Bob Wills is synonymous with western swing. A bandleader, showman, fiddler, singer, and songwriter, he helped create and popularize a form of dance music that blended big band jazz, blues, traditional fiddle tunes, mariachi music, and ragtime. His band, the Texas Playboys, showcased several of country music's most influential musicians.

1969

GENE AUTRY

b. September 29, 1907; d. October 2, 1998 ▪ Tioga, Texas

Hollywood's first famous singing cowboy, Gene Autry ranked as the best-selling country artist from the Depression through World War II. Through his screen roles and as a radio show host, he introduced a romanticized form of western music to the nation. A successful businessman, he was a longtime owner of the Los Angeles Angels baseball team.

1970

CARTER FAMILY

Formed 1927 in Clinch Valley, Virginia

"The first family of country music," the Carter Family ranks among the genre's most popular early acts. A.P. Carter, his wife Sara Carter, and her cousin Maybelle Carter popularized an influential form of harmony singing, and Maybelle's guitar-picking style proved so important that it became known as the "Carter scratch."

BILL MONROE

b. September 13, 1911; d. September 9, 1996 ▪ Rosine, Kentucky

The nickname "The Father of Bluegrass" aptly describes Bill Monroe's role as the founder of an intense, tightly arranged, harmony-rich form of stringband music laced with blues and gospel influences. A powerful mandolinist, Monroe sang in a tight-throated tenor that defined the genre's high, lonesome sound.

1971

ART SATHERLEY

b. October 19, 1889; d. February 10, 1986 ▪ Bristol, England

Art Satherley ranks among early country music's most important record executives. A producer, talent scout, salesman, and manufacturing supervisor, he sought out country and blues artists, working with Roy Acuff, Gene Autry, Spade Cooley, Vernon Dalhart, Al Dexter, Red Foley, Bill Monroe, Tex Ritter, Bob Wills, and other leading country music artists.

1972

JIMMIE DAVIS

b. September 11, 1899; d. November 5, 2000 ▪ Beech Springs, Louisiana

In the 1930s and 1940s, Jimmie Davis's smooth vocal approach helped popularize country music beyond its rural southern audience. His best-selling songs—including "You Are My Sunshine" and "Nobody's Darling but Mine"—not only made him a star but also helped him win roles in Hollywood films and two terms as governor of Louisiana.

1973

CHET ATKINS

b. June 20, 1924; d. June 30, 2001 ▪ Luttrell, Tennessee

No single country instrumentalist achieved the acclaim and respect that Chet Atkins did. His innovative guitar work influenced country, rock, and jazz musicians. He also made his mark as a record producer and RCA executive, running the label's Nashville office from 1955 to 1973 and producing dozens of classic country hits.

PATSY CLINE

b. September 8, 1932; d. March 5, 1963 ▪ Winchester, Virginia

Although popular in her time, Patsy Cline achieved iconic status after a plane crash tragically ended her life. Her rich alto voice, with its impeccable phrasing and emotional expressiveness, has come to set the standard for vocalists in country music and beyond. A 1985 biographical film, *Sweet Dreams*, helped spread her fame.

1974

OWEN BRADLEY

b. October 21, 1915; d. January 7, 1998 ▪ Westmoreland, Tennessee

Owen Bradley was an architect of the Nashville Sound, built one of the first entertainment businesses on what became Music Row, and produced hits with more than a half dozen members of the Country Music Hall of Fame. Bradley ran Decca Records' Nashville division from 1958 to 1976.

PEE WEE KING

b. February 18, 1914; d. March 7, 2000 ▪ Milwaukee, Wisconsin

Pee Wee King became a country music star while including waltzes, polkas, and western music in his repertoire. His band, the Golden West Cowboys, at various times included such important country music figures as Eddy Arnold, Cowboy Copas, Minnie Pearl, Redd Stewart, and Ernest Tubb. He also co-wrote the crossover classic "Tennessee Waltz."

1975

MINNIE PEARL

b. October 25, 1912; d. January 7, 1998 ▪ Centerville, Tennessee

Minnie Pearl (Sarah Colley Cannon) was the queen of country comedy. She became a Grand Ole Opry fixture portraying a flirtatious spinster who joked about her rural hometown, the fictional Grinder's Switch. Her trademarks included a straw hat adorned with a $1.98 price tag and her cheerful greeting, "How-dee! I'm just so proud to be here."

1976

PAUL COHEN

b. November 10, 1908; d. April 1, 1970 ▪ Chicago, Illinois

Paul Cohen, head of Decca Records' country department from the mid-1940s to 1958, played a major role in Nashville's emergence as a country music recording capital. Based in New York, Cohen began recording Decca stars Red Foley and Ernest Tubb in Nashville by 1947, when he hired producer Owen Bradley to help him oversee Decca's country music roster.

Eddy Arnold is presented with his Country Music Hall of Fame plaque, 1966. Future Hall of Fame member Jo Walker-Meador is at far right.

KITTY WELLS

b. August 30, 1919; d. July 16, 2012 ▪ Nashville, Tennessee

Kitty Wells was thirty-three and contemplating retirement in 1952 when her breakthrough hit, "It Wasn't God Who Made Honky Tonk Angels," made her a star. Her piercing, intensely honest vocal style and the down-to-earth themes of her songs resonated with audiences and broke barriers for female country singers.

1977

MERLE TRAVIS

b. November 29, 1917; d. October 20, 1983 ▪ Rosewood, Kentucky

A backwoods renaissance man, Merle Travis was an innovative guitarist, songwriter, and vocalist, as well as a guitar designer, cartoonist, and author. He wrote many country hits, including "Sixteen Tons" and "Dark as a Dungeon," and profoundly influenced several generations of musicians, including Chet Atkins.

1978

GRANDPA JONES

b. October 20, 1913; d. February 19, 1998 ▪ Niagara, Kentucky

An exuberant banjoist, vocalist, and comedian, Grandpa Jones was a dedicated champion of old-time music. He continued to play clawhammer banjo when others shifted toward the three-finger style popularized by Earl Scruggs, and his roles on the Grand Ole Opry, *Hee Haw*, and in gospel quartets kept country music connected to its early roots.

1979

HUBERT LONG

b. December 3, 1923; d. September 7, 1972 ▪ Poteet, Texas

A leading Nashville talent promoter, artist manager, and music publisher, Hubert Long was a top country music executive in the 1950s and 1960s. The Hubert Long Agency became one of Nashville's first independent talent agencies, and he was a founding board member of the Country Music Association and the Country Music Hall of Fame and Museum.

Country Music Hall of Fame members Porter Wagoner, Jim Foglesong, and Kris Kristofferson at the 2003 Medallion Ceremony.

HANK SNOW

b. May 9, 1914; d. December 20, 1999 ▪ Brooklyn, Nova Scotia, Canada

Hank Snow combined a distinctive vocal style and songwriting gifts to establish himself as one of the biggest country stars in the years following World War II. An accomplished guitarist as well, he experimented with Latin rhythms, jazz, blues, Hawaiian music, and gospel songs, giving them all an individual touch of his own.

1980

JOHNNY CASH

b. February 26, 1932; d. September 12, 2003 ▪ Kingsland, Arkansas

An international ambassador for country music, Johnny Cash connected with prisoners and presidents, and with rebels and religious figures. He developed a starkly minimalist sound with his band, the Tennessee Two, which framed his deep, authoritative voice, leading to an enduring career including success as an actor, author, and network TV host.

CONNIE B. GAY

b. August 22, 1914; d. December 4, 1989 ▪ Lizard Lick, North Carolina

Dubbed country music's Media Magician, Connie B. Gay became a leading country music entrepreneur. Working out of Washington, D.C., in the 1950s and 1960s, Gay organized radio, TV, and stage shows that helped turn rural-based country music into an all-American form of modern entertainment.

SONS OF THE PIONEERS

Formed 1933 in Los Angeles, California

America's premier western vocal group, the Sons of the Pioneers drew on cowboy themes and featured three-part harmonies and stellar instrumental work. Original members included Roy Rogers, who went on to solo fame as a singer and actor, as well as ace songwriters Bob Nolan and Tim Spencer, and brothers Hugh and Karl Farr.

1981

VERNON DALHART

b. April 6, 1883; d. September 14, 1948 ▪ Jefferson, Texas

Vernon Dalhart, an operatically trained singer, became one of the most productive and versatile performers in early country music. His 1924 recording of "The Wreck of the Old '97" coupled with "The Prisoner's Song" is credited as country music's first million seller. His clear diction helped make down-home country material accessible to broad audiences, both rural and urban.

GRANT TURNER

b. May 17, 1912; d. October 19, 1991 ▪ Baird, Texas

Grant Turner, known as the Voice of the Grand Ole Opry, served on the show's announcing staff for forty-seven years and became a broadcasting icon. Beloved for his warm manner, careful diction, and ingratiating personality, Turner was one of three original members elected to the Country Disc Jockey Hall of Fame.

1982

LEFTY FRIZZELL

b. March 31, 1928; d. July 19, 1975 ▪ Corsicana, Texas

Lefty Frizzell, known for his vowel-bending phrasing and intimate vocal tone, ranks among the most influential performers in country music history. His distinctive style helped shape the artistry of Merle Haggard, George Jones, George Strait, Randy Travis, and Keith Whitley. Frizzell enjoyed a run of top hits in the 1950s and continued recording until his death.

ROY HORTON

b. November 5, 1914; d. September 23, 2003 ▪ Broad Top, Pennsylvania

After performing in the Hilltoppers with his brother Vaughan, Roy Horton spent forty years as an important executive with Peer-Southern Music, a top country music publishing company. A CMA stalwart, he developed the catalogs of the Carter Family, Ted Daffan, Jimmie Davis, Bill Monroe, Jimmie Rodgers, Floyd Tillman, and other country greats.

MARTY ROBBINS

b. September 26, 1925; d. December 8, 1982 ▪ near Glendale, Arizona

Marty Robbins achieved success as a recording artist, stage performer, songwriter, TV program host, actor, author, and stock car racer. The versatile singer applied his supple voice to country, gospel, Hawaiian, pop, rockabilly, and western material. A fan favorite, his midnight performances on the Grand Ole Opry became a long-running tradition.

1983

LITTLE JIMMY DICKENS

b. December 19, 1920 d. January 2, 2015 ▪ Bolt, West Virginia

Little Jimmy Dickens's big voice and brassy style—paired with his physical stature of four feet, eleven inches—made him a favorite with country fans. Starting in 1949, he first made his reputation with a string of novelty songs, but soon proved to be a versatile entertainer who delivered tear-filled ballads and rockabilly tunes with equal effectiveness.

1984

RALPH PEER

b. May 22, 1892; d. January 19, 1960 ▪ Kansas City, Missouri

Ralph Peer was the most prominent businessman in early country music. Indeed, his impact on the larger popular music industry—as a pioneer in recording, music publishing, and artist management—is incalculable. Among other accomplishments, he discovered the Carter Family and Jimmie Rodgers and steered their rise to prominence.

FLOYD TILLMAN

b. December 8, 1914; d. August 22, 2003 ▪ Ryan, Oklahoma

In the 1930s and 1940s, singer-songwriter Floyd Tillman contributed to the rise of western swing and honky-tonk music while penning country standards. His songwriting catalog includes early crossover hits, such as "It Makes No Difference Now," "I Love You So Much It Hurts," and "Slippin' Around."

Country Music Hall of Fame inductees Jean Shepard, Bobby Braddock, and Reba McEntire, 2011.

1985

FLATT & SCRUGGS

Formed 1948 in Nashville, Tennessee

Flatt & Scruggs helped popularize bluegrass music in the 1950s and 1960s. Singer-guitarist Lester Flatt and banjoist extraordinaire Earl Scruggs joined Bill Monroe & His Blue Grass Boys in 1945, leaving in 1948 and forming their own band soon after. Their syndicated TV show and other work on TV and movie soundtracks spread their fame worldwide.

1986

THE DUKE OF PADUCAH

b. May 12, 1901; d. June 20, 1986 ▪ DeSoto, Missouri

Benjamin "Whitey" Ford was a leading country comedian from the 1930s to the 1950s. He acquired his stage moniker, the Duke of Paducah, while broadcasting on St. Louis radio station KWK. He helped organize the *Renfro Valley Barn Dance* and starred for years on the Grand Ole Opry's network segment.

WESLEY ROSE

b. February 11, 1918; d. April 26, 1990 ▪ Chicago, Illinois

Wesley Rose joined Acuff-Rose Publications in 1945 at the invitation of his father, Fred Rose, and later became one of the world's top music-publishing executives. After his father's death in 1954, Rose became the firm's president, as well as head of Hickory Records. He later launched the Acuff-Rose Artists Corporation and became a successful record producer.

1987

ROD BRASFIELD

b. August 22, 1910; d. September 12, 1958 ▪ Smithville, Mississippi

From 1947 to 1958, Grand Ole Opry star Rod Brasfield was a premier country music comedian. His trademark baggy suit, button shoes, beat-up hat, rubbery face, and clacking false teeth would have audiences laughing before he spoke. Brasfield also starred in the 1957 film *A Face in the Crowd*.

1988

LORETTA LYNN

b. April 14, 1932; d. October 4, 2022 ▪ Butcher Holler, Kentucky

Despite growing up in poverty, marrying in her mid-teens, and having four children by age twenty, Loretta Lynn became one of country's most popular performers. Assertive, autobiographical songs, including "You Ain't Woman Enough" and "Don't Come Home a-Drinkin' (with Lovin' on Your Mind)," broke ground for female singer-songwriters. Her 1978 autobiography, *Coal Miner's Daughter*, became an award-winning film.

ROY ROGERS

b. November 5, 1911; d. July 6, 1998 ▪ Cincinnati, Ohio

Roy Rogers earned the title King of the Cowboys by succeeding Gene Autry as America's most popular western film star. Before beginning his movie career and starring with wife Dale Evans on film and TV, Rogers was a founding member of western vocal group the Sons of the Pioneers.

1989

JACK STAPP

b. December 8, 1912; d. December 20, 1980 ▪ Nashville, Tennessee

Jack Stapp made country music history in two executive posts. As WSM radio's program director from 1939 to 1957, he signed such artists as Red Foley, Carl Smith, Hank Snow, and Hank Williams to the Grand Ole Opry. In 1951, Stapp also founded the enormously successful Tree Publishing Company, later bought by Sony Music.

CLIFFIE STONE

b. March 1, 1917; d. January 17, 1998 ▪ Stockton, California

Over six decades, Cliffie Stone contributed to country music as a radio and TV personality, recording artist, bass player, record producer, talent scout, song publisher, and artist manager. All of those roles made him a pivotal figure in the development of California's post-war country music scene.

HANK THOMPSON

b. September 3, 1925; d. November 6, 2007 ▪ Waco, Texas

Hank Thompson created a distinctive blend of honky-tonk and western swing that gave him a lengthy career and helped keep these traditions alive during the rise of rock & roll and country's experimentation with rock and pop. Between 1948 and 1974, Thompson scored twenty-eight Top Ten hits and continued to chart into the 1980s.

1990

TENNESSEE ERNIE FORD

b. February 13, 1919; d. October 17, 1991 ▪ Bristol, Tennessee

With a resonant baritone and good-natured humor, Tennessee Ernie Ford gained success as a recording artist, actor, comedian, and TV host. Besides releasing crossover hits such as "Sixteen Tons," Ford recorded a series of popular gospel albums. He hosted several NBC-TV programs, including a game show and his own variety series.

1991

BOUDLEAUX AND FELICE BRYANT

Married September 5, 1945, in Milwaukee, Wisconsin

Husband and wife Boudleaux and Felice Bryant were among the first in Nashville to make a full-time career of songwriting. They wrote some of the most memorable songs of the 1950s and 1960s, including "Rocky Top" and many hits for the Everly Brothers, such as "Bye Bye Love," "Wake Up, Little Susie," and "All I Have to Do Is Dream."

1992

GEORGE JONES

b. September 12, 1931; d. April 26, 2013 ▪ Saratoga, Texas

George Jones's wide vocal range and his emotive way with lyrics made him one of the most admired country artists in history and a successor to such masterful singers as Hank Williams and Lefty Frizzell. His drama-filled life, with its trials and triumphs, gave his work a realistic feel that cemented his connection with fans.

FRANCES PRESTON

b. August 27, 1928; d. June 13, 2012 ▪ Nashville, Tennessee

Frances Preston rose from working as a receptionist at WSM radio to become one of the most important music business leaders in America. In 1958, her contacts and professionalism led BMI to ask her to open its southern regional office in Nashville. By 1986, she was BMI's president and CEO, based in New York. She retired from BMI in 2004.

1993

WILLIE NELSON

b. April 30, 1933 ▪ Abbott, Texas

One of country music's most versatile and enduring singer-songwriters, Nelson recorded twenty-one #1 hits between 1962 and 1993. But that's only part of the story, as Nelson's restless creativity and boundless energy have resulted in a career that has embraced nearly every genre of American music and featured collaborations with dozens of other artists.

1994

MERLE HAGGARD

b. April 6, 1937; d. April 6, 2016 ▪ Bakersfield, California

With the possible exception of Hank Williams, Merle Haggard is country music's most influential singer-songwriter. He was also one of the genre's most versatile artists, mining honky-tonk, blues, jazz, pop, and folk, yet making all his recordings personal and distinctly his own. He also helped establish Bakersfield, California, as an important country music center.

1995

ROGER MILLER

b. January 2, 1936; d. October 25, 1992 ▪ Fort Worth, Texas

Roger Miller left a musical legacy of astonishing depth and range. First finding success as a songwriter, he exploded in popularity as a Grammy-winning performer in the 1960s with the clever, witty crossover hits "Dang Me," "King of the Road," and "Chug-a-Lug." He won a 1985 Tony Award for his musical score for *Big River.*

JO WALKER-MEADOR

b. February 16, 1924; d. August 16, 2017 ▪ Orlinda, Tennessee

Executive director of the Country Music Association from 1962 to 1991, Jo Walker-Meador facilitated country music's growth as a national radio format. During her tenure at CMA, country assumed a dominant presence in American culture. She led campaigns to establish the Country Music Hall of Fame, the annual CMA awards show, and Fan Fair (now known as CMA Music Festival).

1996

PATSY MONTANA

b. October 30, 1908; d. May 3, 1996 ▪ Hope, Arkansas

Patsy Montana's 1935 recording of "I Wanna Be a Cowboy's Sweetheart" was the first female solo recording to become a runaway hit. With a sparkling voice, spirited yodeling, and signature cowgirl outfits, she sang of love, independence, and the romance of the West—appealing to Depression Era fans in need of cheerful entertainment.

Presentation of Country Music Hall of Fame plaques at the 1973 CMA Awards.

Left to right: Tex Ritter, Chet Atkins, and Roy Acuff.

BUCK OWENS

b. August 12, 1929; d. March 25, 2006 ▪ Sherman, Texas

Singer, songwriter, and guitarist Buck Owens ruled country music in the 1960s. His many hits—energetic, guitar-driven, danceable—helped define the West Coast country sound. He later became a fixture on television as co-host of the long-running syndicated program *Hee Haw*. A highly successful businessman, he oversaw a variety of profitable ventures.

RAY PRICE

b. January 12, 1926; d. December 16, 2013 ▪ Perryville, Texas

Ray Price ranks among country music's most important innovators and one of its most enduring artists. He changed the sound of country music from the late 1950s forward by developing a rhythmic form of honky-tonk that has been a staple of country music ever since. He later recorded lushly orchestrated pop-country ballads that also broke new ground.

1997

HARLAN HOWARD

b. September 8, 1927; d. March 3, 2002 ▪ Detroit, Michigan

Harlan Howard stands as the archetype of the professional Nashville songwriter. Arriving in Nashville in 1960 after penning hits for Ray Price and Charlie Walker, he approached songwriting as a daily job and wrote dozens of country classics across the decades, from Patsy Cline's "I Fall to Pieces" to the Judds' "Why Not Me."

BRENDA LEE

b. December 11, 1944 ▪ Atlanta, Georgia

Brenda Lee ranks among America's most talented singers, and her immense success as a pop artist, along with Elvis Presley and the Everly Brothers, helped make Nashville an all-purpose recording center. As rock overtook pop on the charts, Lee turned to country music in the 1970s and gained hits into the 1980s.

Brenda Lee with her Country Music Hall of Fame plaque, 1997.

CINDY WALKER

b. July 20, 1917; d. March 23, 2006 ▪ Mart, Texas

Cindy Walker became one of country music's finest songwriters through a knack for tailoring songs for a diverse list of stylists, including Eddy Arnold, Gene Autry, Hank Snow, and Bob Wills. Her Top Ten hits spanned a half century, ranging from "Cherokee Maiden" to "You Don't Know Me" to "Dream Baby (How Long Must I Dream)."

1998

GEORGE MORGAN

b. June 29, 1924; d. July 7, 1975 ▪ Waverly, Tennessee

George Morgan's smooth tenor made him a fixture on the Grand Ole Opry for decades. In 1949, he had five singles simultaneously in the country Top Ten, including his signature hit, "Candy Kisses." Morgan hosted a Nashville TV show in the 1950s and, in 1973, introduced his daughter Lorrie Morgan for her Grand Ole Opry debut.

ELVIS PRESLEY

b. January 8, 1935; d. August 16, 1977 ▪ Tupelo, Mississippi

Elvis Presley remains rock & roll's most important figure, but he initially set out to be a country singer, and several of his early songs came from the genre. He later recorded country music, and his impact on the genre was immense, helping it move from a regional phenomenon to national status.

E.W. "BUD" WENDELL

b. August 17, 1927 ▪ Akron, Ohio

Bud Wendell advanced country music in several executive roles: longtime manager of the Grand Ole Opry; president and CEO of the company that owned the Opry and the Opryland hotel and theme park; and developer of the cable TV networks TNN and CMT. He also was board chairman of the Country Music Hall of Fame and Museum for many years.

TAMMY WYNETTE

b. May 5, 1942; d. April 6, 1998 ▪ Itawamba County, Mississippi

On record and on stage, Tammy Wynette paired southern dignity with country grit. A former hairdresser, she cultivated a glamorous appearance and sang with an omnipresent tear and twang in her voice. Her songs dealt with the romantic ideals and difficulties of family-oriented women, both as a soloist and in her duets with third husband George Jones.

1999

JOHNNY BOND

b. June 1, 1915; d. June 12, 1978 ▪ Enville, Oklahoma

Johnny Bond was an important western music songwriter and performer. He composed hundreds of songs, including such classics as "Cimarron," "I Wonder Where You Are Tonight," and "Tomorrow Never Comes." He also was an actor, author, a regular on California-based TV and radio programs, and a music publisher with business partner Tex Ritter.

DOLLY PARTON

b. January 19, 1946 ▪ Sevier County, Tennessee

Dolly Parton's striking artistry and image helped revolutionize the world of country music for female performers. In 1967, she had her first solo hit and became Porter Wagoner's duet partner on recordings, on stage, and on his syndicated TV series. Going solo in 1974, she recorded pop hits, starred on TV and in films, and opened an East Tennessee theme park.

CONWAY TWITTY

b. September 1, 1933; d. June 5, 1993 ▪ Friars Point, Mississippi

During his lifetime, Conway Twitty had more #1 records than any country artist to that point. A diverse stylist and significant songwriter, he experienced his first success with the 1958 pop hit "It's Only Make Believe" before turning to country music in the 1960s. Twitty also recorded a series of famous duets with Loretta Lynn.

2000

CHARLEY PRIDE

b. March 18, 1934; d. December 12, 2020 ▪ Sledge, Mississippi

Charley Pride overcame barriers of racial prejudice and segregation to become a leading country star. His warm baritone voice first hit country radio in 1966, and he continued enjoying hits for more than twenty years. Pride also proved to be an astute businessman, investing in real estate and banking from his home in Dallas.

FARON YOUNG

b. February 25, 1932; d. December 10, 1996 ▪ Shreveport, Louisiana

From the 1950s through the 1970s, Faron Young was a leading country star and one of the genre's most colorful personalities. He recorded hits as a honky-tonker and as a sensitive balladeer, and, on the side, he became a magazine publisher and real estate investor.

2001

BILL ANDERSON

b. November 1, 1937 ▪ Columbia, South Carolina

Among country music's most successful singer-songwriters, Bill Anderson recorded thirty-seven Top Ten singles between 1960 and 1978, and he has written country hits for more than fifty years. His breathy, conversational tenor earned him the nickname "Whisperin' Bill." In addition, he has worked as an actor, fronted a syndicated TV music program, and hosted TV game shows.

DELMORE BROTHERS

Formed circa 1931 in Elkmont, Alabama

The Delmore Brothers, Alton and Rabon, were arguably the most musically sophisticated and technically proficient of the many great brother duos of the 1930s and 1940s. Their soft, pliant harmony, dazzling guitar work, love of blues, and well-crafted songs endeared them to generations of fans. Several of their hits—including "Brown's Ferry Blues" and "Blues Stay Away from Me"—became country standards.

EVERLY BROTHERS

Formed circa 1954 in Kentucky

The Everly Brothers, Don and Phil, were one of popular music's most successful acts between 1957 and 1962. They also were important to Nashville, as they were the city's first consistently successful rock & roll act. Their management and songs came from Nashville, and they recorded with local studio musicians. They split in 1973 and reunited ten years later.

Kitty Wells with her Country Music Hall of Fame plaque, 1976.

DON GIBSON

b. April 3, 1928; d. November 17, 2003 ▪ Shelby, North Carolina

Masterful songwriter and performer Don Gibson composed three of country music's most famous songs: "Sweet Dreams," "Oh Lonesome Me," and "I Can't Stop Loving You." He also released more than seventy charted singles between 1956 and 1980, and his recordings, produced by Chet Atkins, helped define the musical style known as the Nashville Sound.

HOMER & JETHRO

Formed 1936 in Knoxville, Tennessee

Famous for their song satires, dry comic delivery, and instrumental virtuosity, Homer & Jethro (Henry "Homer" Haynes and Kenneth "Jethro" Burns) were country music's most beloved musical comedy act of the 1950s and 1960s. Their success took them from radio barn dances to network television variety shows, urban nightclubs, and Las Vegas showrooms.

WAYLON JENNINGS

b. June 15, 1937; d. February 13, 2002 ▪ Littlefield, Texas

Waylon Jennings worked in radio, played in Buddy Holly's band, roomed with Johnny Cash, and acted in a 1967 film, *Nashville Rebel*, before he became a music star. Jennings grew into a musical hero in the early 1970s when he assumed artistic control of his albums and helped create what became known as the Outlaw movement.

JORDANAIRES

Formed 1948 in Springfield, Missouri

Nashville's premier background vocal group, the Jordanaires established themselves as a gospel quartet before they won fame for their studio work. Elvis Presley invited the group to back him starting in 1956, which led to a long association with Presley and a lengthy run as a renowned harmony act, on their own and behind other vocalists.

George Strait and Bill Anderson, 2007 Medallion Ceremony.

DON LAW

b. February 24, 1902; d. December 20, 1982 ▪ London, England

The head of Columbia Records' country music division from 1952 to 1967, Don Law was one of the most successful producers in the annals of country music. He worked with stars Johnny Cash, Lefty Frizzell, Johnny Horton, Ray Price, and Carl Smith—gaining their respect for letting them forge their own sounds.

LOUVIN BROTHERS

Formed 1942 in Henegar, Alabama

Ira and Charlie Louvin of the Louvin Brothers were the link between early brother duets such as the Delmore Brothers and the more modern Everly Brothers. Moreover, the Louvins' stratospheric vocal interplay made them one of country music's most influential acts of any era. Charlie Louvin established a solo career after splitting from Ira, who died in 1965.

KEN NELSON

b. January 19, 1911; d. January 6, 2008 ▪ Caledonia, Minnesota

Ken Nelson handled A&R for the country division of Capitol Records from 1951 to 1969, helping give country music a national presence after World War II. Nelson was considered an artist-friendly record producer, who encouraged Merle Haggard, Wanda Jackson, Buck Owens, Faron Young, and others to develop styles of their own.

SAM PHILLIPS

b. January 5, 1923; d. July 30, 2004 ▪ Florence, Alabama

One of American music's most important figures, Sam Phillips founded Sun Records and introduced the world to Johnny Cash, Jerry Lee Lewis, Roy Orbison, Carl Perkins, Elvis Presley, and Charlie Rich. By seeking artists with style and vision, and by recording them as spontaneously as possible, he captured distinctive sounds that launched legendary careers.

WEBB PIERCE

b. August 8, 1921; d. February 24, 1991 ▪ West Monroe, Louisiana

Webb Pierce was one of country music's biggest stars in the 1950s—and one of its most flamboyant, with his flashy Nudie-tailored suits and custom cars. Pierce's high, piercing tenor gave him an instantly identifiable voice, and his knack for recognizing a good country song led to thirteen #1 singles in the 1950s.

2002

BILL CARLISLE

b. December 19, 1908; d. March 17, 2003 ▪ Wakefield, Kentucky

A top showman and talented songwriter, Bill Carlisle joined the first generation of country performers in the 1920s and was still performing his mix of blues-influenced, old-time country and novelty songs in the twenty-first century. He first performed with his brother Cliff, and for more than fifty years led a family group, the Carlisles.

PORTER WAGONER

b. August 12, 1927; d. October 28, 2007 ▪ Howell County, Missouri

Porter Wagoner became one of country music's most enduring and recognizable stars. Wagoner's achievements included eighty-one chart records—including several country standards. He served as a beloved TV program host and an expert showman easily identified by his blond pompadour, rhinestone suits, and down-home humor. After Roy Acuff's death, Wagoner served as the unofficial spokesman for the Grand Ole Opry.

2003

FLOYD CRAMER

b. October 27, 1933; d. December 31, 1997 ▪ Shreveport, Louisiana

Floyd Cramer became one of the busiest musicians in Nashville once the piano became an integral instrument in country arrangements starting in the late 1950s. He popularized the slip-note technique, a popular feature of country recordings, and his tasteful playing was heard on his own instrumental hits, such as "Last Date" and "San Antonio Rose."

CARL SMITH

b. March 15, 1927; d. January 16, 2010 ▪ Maynardville, Tennessee

Carl Smith stands as one of country's most popular hitmakers in the 1950s and 1960s. Influenced by Roy Acuff and Hank Williams, the tall, handsome singer developed a hard-edged sound that he presented with easy confidence. He co-hosted the nationally televised *Five Star Jubilee* program and for five years hosted a Canadian program, *Carl Smith's Country Music Hall.*

2004

JIM FOGLESONG

b. July 26, 1922; d. July 9, 2013 ▪ Lundale, West Virginia

As a producer and record label executive, Jim Foglesong advanced the careers of many country acts while inspiring associates with his high ethical standards. After success as a pop producer, Foglesong moved to Nashville in 1970 as A&R chief for Dot Records. He later headed the local offices of the ABC-Dot, MCA, and Capitol labels.

KRIS KRISTOFFERSON

b. June 22, 1936; d. September 28, 2024 ▪ Brownsville, Texas

Few songwriters have exerted more influence on country music or have been as successful beyond the limits of Music Row as Kris Kristofferson. Since the 1960s, Kristofferson has excelled as a recording artist and Hollywood actor, and as a songwriter, he established standards that continue to set the bar for others in his field.

2005

ALABAMA

Formed 1973 in Fort Payne, Alabama

Alabama greatly influenced country music's popularity during the band's heyday, from the 1980s into the 1990s. The family-based act—Randy Owen on vocals and guitar, Jeff Cook on guitar, Teddy Gentry on bass, Mark Herndon on drums—had thirty-two #1 country hits, sold millions of albums, and proved that a self-contained band could achieve top sales and status in country music.

Little Jimmy Dickens and Carl Smith at the 2003 Medallion Ceremony.

DeFORD BAILEY

b. December 14, 1899; d. July 2, 1982 ▪ Smith County, Tennessee

DeFord Bailey was the first Black star of the Grand Ole Opry and one of its most popular early performers. Dubbed "The Harmonica Wizard," Bailey recorded for the Brunswick and Victor labels; his Victor recordings took place during the first recording sessions held in Nashville by a major label. He also toured widely, despite the Jim Crow laws of the time.

GLEN CAMPBELL

b. April 22, 1936; d. August 8, 2017 ▪ Delight, Arkansas

A gifted singer and guitarist, Glen Campbell rose to stardom with a string of pop-country hits in the 1960s and 1970s. At his peak, Campbell hosted *The Glen Campbell Goodtime Hour*, a CBS-TV variety show, from 1968 to 1972. He also starred in several movies, including *True Grit* with John Wayne.

2006

HAROLD BRADLEY

b. January 2, 1926; d. January 31, 2019 ▪ Nashville, Tennessee

The "Dean of the Nashville Session Guitarists," Harold Bradley played his first recording session in 1946, with Pee Wee King. Subsequently, he played on hundreds of hit recordings, for everyone from Eddy Arnold and Red Foley to Elvis Presley and Roy Orbison. He headed the Nashville Chapter of the American Federation of Musicians from 1991 to 2008.

SONNY JAMES

b. May 1, 1928; d. February 22, 2016 ▪ Hackleburg, Alabama

Sonny James enjoyed one of country music's most distinguished careers. Between 1953 and 1983, he amassed seventy-two chart records, twenty-three of which went to #1. Known as the "Southern Gentleman" for his gracious manner, James enjoyed his greatest success singing romantic ballads. He also worked as a producer, helping Marie Osmond with her #1 crossover hit, "Paper Roses."

GEORGE STRAIT

b. May 18, 1952 ▪ Poteet, Texas

George Strait arrived as a Texas traditionalist amid a contemporary country scene in which pop-crossover sounds prevailed. Bucking convention, he went on to become one of the most successful, enduring, and influential recording artists of his time. He has had more than ninety chart hits and more #1s than any other artist in country music history.

2007

RALPH EMERY

b. March 10, 1933; d. January 15, 2022 ▪ McEwen, Tennessee

Ralph Emery ranks as one of the most famous radio and TV personalities in country music. The longtime WSM radio deejay hosted the popular TNN prime-time talk show, *Nashville Now*, as well as long-running syndicated programs (*Pop Goes the Country, Nashville Alive*) and a daily morning Nashville TV program, *The Ralph Emery Show*.

Tom T. Hall at the 2008 Medallion Ceremony.

VINCE GILL

b. April 12, 1957 ▪ Norman, Oklahoma

Vince Gill is one of the most awarded country stars of his era, thanks to his aching tenor voice, his songwriting skills, and his virtuoso guitar chops. Besides registering a long string of hits, he hosted the CMA Awards from 1992 to 2003, and his easygoing demeanor and devotion to charitable causes have made him one of country music's best-liked insiders.

MEL TILLIS

b. August 8, 1932; d. November 19, 2017 ▪ Pahokee, Florida

Mel Tillis parlayed his success as a respected Nashville songwriter in the 1950s and 1960s into a substantial recording and touring career that flourished in the 1970s and beyond. A chronic stutterer, Tillis used this challenge to enhance an affable, down-home comic persona that resulted in film roles and a strong TV presence.

2008

TOM T. HALL

b. May 25, 1936; d. August 20, 2021 ▪ Olive Hill, Kentucky

Tom T. Hall was among the leading songwriters who, in the 1960s and 1970s, imbued country music with a new level of lyric and thematic sophistication and social consciousness, while maintaining the music's inherent rusticity and simplicity of form. Known as "The Storyteller," Hall flourished as a recording artist with original, poignant, sometimes sardonic musical slices of life.

EMMYLOU HARRIS

b. April 2, 1947 ▪ Birmingham, Alabama

Emmylou Harris has stretched beyond the conventional parameters of country, bluegrass, and rock, yet she honors those genres by tapping into their most emotionally stirring qualities. She began achieving hits while in California, appealing to rock and country crowds, and after moving to Nashville and onto the country charts, she continued to experiment and to attract diverse audiences.

STATLER BROTHERS

Formed 1961 in Staunton, Virginia

The Statler Brothers presented a combination of musical talent, showmanship, and humor, creating a career that lasted more than half a century. Influenced by gospel quartets, the vocal group included Harold Reid, his brother Don Reid, Phil Balsley, and Lew Dewitt. Health issues led Dewitt to leave in 1982, replaced by Jimmy Fortune.

ERNEST V. "POP" STONEMAN

b. May 25, 1893; d. June 14, 1968 ▪ Monarat, Virginia

Patriarch of a successful musical family, Pop Stoneman helped establish country music's validity during the 1920s. He hit his stride as an artist in 1925, recording event songs, sentimental tunes, and gospel standards. The Great Depression ended his early career, but he returned after World War II leading his children in the Stoneman Family band.

2009

ROY CLARK

b. April 15, 1933; d. November 15, 2018 ▪ Meherrin, Virginia

An all-around entertainer, Roy Clark was a singer and masterful guitarist whose range as a showman included playing a pickin' and grinnin' bumpkin on TV and in movies as well as performing with symphony orchestras; headlining in Las Vegas; running his own theater in Branson, Missouri; and serving as a recurring guest host on *The Tonight Show*.

BARBARA MANDRELL

b. December 15, 1948 ▪ Houston, Texas

Few entertainers have been as hard-working or as multi-talented as Barbara Mandrell. A seasoned pro who could play several instruments by age fourteen, she was a hit recording artist at twenty-one. She went on to star on network television as host of a variety show and to headline in Las Vegas.

Charlie McCoy, Barbara Mandrell, and Roy Clark at the 2009 Medallion Ceremony.

CHARLIE McCOY

b. March 28, 1941 ▪ Oak Hill, West Virginia

The most recorded harmonica player in history, Charlie McCoy has graced the recordings of artists ranging from Elvis Presley and Bob Dylan to George Jones and Loretta Lynn. His musicianship is distinguished by its speed, precision, clarity, phrasing, and emotional depth. McCoy is almost single-handedly responsible for re-establishing the harmonica as a popular instrument in country music.

Singing "Will the Circle Be Unbroken" at the conclusion of the 2012 Medallion Ceremony.

Left to right: Emmylou Harris, Crystal Gayle, Bobby Braddock, Brenda Lee, James Taylor, Barbara Mandrell, Harold Bradley, Connie Smith, Roy Clark, Sonny James (obscured), Merle Haggard, Jo Walker-Meador, and Ralph Emery.

2010

JIMMY DEAN

b. August 10, 1928; d. June 13, 2010 ▪ Olton, Texas

Jimmy Dean's affable charm and fresh-faced looks epitomized the country TV star of the 1950s. Though Dean was able to parlay his specialty, the dramatic narrative, into a string of hit records in the 1960s, he gained his biggest success as the host of televised variety shows, as a fill-in host of network talk shows, and as an actor in TV and film.

FERLIN HUSKY

b. December 3, 1925; d. March 17, 2011 ▪ Cantwell, Missouri

Entertainer extraordinaire Ferlin Husky started in Southern California as a radio host, a television regular, and a country hitmaker as well as a comedian who performed under a hayseed alter ego, Simon Crum. By 1956, Husky recorded in Music City, with his 1957 hit "Gone" credited as the beginning of the polished Nashville Sound. He continued to chart hits into the 1970s.

BILLY SHERRILL

b. November 5, 1936; d. August 4, 2015 ▪ Phil Campbell, Alabama

One of the most influential producers in history, Billy Sherrill helped shape the evolving sound of country music, especially in the 1970s. Every artist he worked with prospered under his visionary direction, including George Jones, Tammy Wynette, Charlie Rich, Tanya Tucker, Barbara Mandrell, David Houston, and Johnny Paycheck.

DON WILLIAMS

b. May 27, 1939; d. September 8, 2017 ▪ Floydada, Texas

Nicknamed the "Gentle Giant" for his height and his laid-back baritone voice, Don Williams enjoyed an enduring career, scoring at least one big hit every year between 1974 and 1991. He achieved enormous success overseas, aided by classics such as the pulsing up-tempo tune "Tulsa Time" and the reflective gem "Good Ole Boys Like Me."

2011

BOBBY BRADDOCK

b. August 5, 1940 ▪ Lakeland, Florida

One of Nashville's most admired and inventive songwriters, Bobby Braddock landed his first cut in 1966 and eventually penned such country classics as Tammy Wynette's "D-I-V-O-R-C-E" and George Jones's "He Stopped Loving Her Today," both cowritten with Curly Putman. Decades later, Braddock had hits with Tracy Lawrence, Toby Keith, and Billy Currington.

REBA McENTIRE

b. March 28, 1955 ▪ McAlester, Oklahoma

Reba McEntire is the most successful female performer of her generation, and she has been cited as a role model by nearly every female country singer to follow. She has had more #1 country albums than any female singer in history, and she also succeeded as an author, a businesswoman, and an actor on Broadway, on film, and on TV.

JEAN SHEPARD

b. November 1, 1933; d. September 25, 2016 ▪ Pauls Valley, Oklahoma

Jean Shepard was one of the few women to become country stars in the 1950s, and even rarer, she did so with feisty honky-tonk songs and candid material. Her lively style set the stage for the breakthroughs of Loretta Lynn, Dolly Parton, and Tammy Wynette, and she continued to gain hit records into the 1970s.

2012

GARTH BROOKS

b. February 7, 1962 ▪ Luba, Oklahoma

Garth Brooks emerged in the 1990s to become one of the biggest-selling music acts of all time. In the process, he helped move country into the mainstream of American entertainment. After selling more than 100 million albums, he announced his retirement in 2000 to raise his children. He staged periodic concerts and occasionally released new records before fully resuming his career in 2014.

Vince Gill performs at the 2014 Medallion Ceremony.

HARGUS "PIG" ROBBINS

b. January 18, 1938; d. January 30, 2022 ▪ Rhea County, Tennessee

Blind pianist Pig Robbins succeeded Floyd Cramer as the leading session keyboardist in Nashville, from the mid-1960s through the 1980s. Robbins's first hit session yielded George Jones's "White Lightning," and he went on to record with rockers (Bob Dylan and Neil Young) as well as dozens of country hitmakers (such as Crystal Gayle, Charlie Rich, Randy Travis, and Alan Jackson).

CONNIE SMITH

b. August 14, 1941 ▪ Elkhart, Indiana

Connie Smith shot to stardom with her first release, the #1 hit "Once a Day." Her expressive voice offered an exceptional combination of tone, power, phrasing, and emotion, but her greatness extends beyond vocal brilliance. It encompasses her song selection, her connection to great musicians, her classy demeanor, and a spiritual bearing that serves as her foundation.

2013

BOBBY BARE

b. April 7, 1935 ▪ Lawrence County, Ohio

Bobby Bare is a storyteller, humorist, folk singer, and outlaw, with a keen instinct for good songs. He championed the early work of Rodney Crowell, Tom T. Hall, Kris Kristofferson, Bob McDill, Mickey Newbury, Billy Joe Shaver, and Shel Silverstein, helping country music evolve with the times. He also hosted the acclaimed television show *Bobby Bare and Friends* in the 1980s.

JACK CLEMENT

b. April 5, 1931; d. August 8, 2013 ▪ Whitehaven, Tennessee

Known as "Cowboy," Jack Clement ranks among the most important producers, songwriters, and entrepreneurs in country music history. He joined Sun Records in 1954 in Memphis, where he recorded Johnny Cash, Jerry Lee Lewis, Carl Perkins, and Roy Orbison. Clement moved to Nashville in 1960, where he owned recording studios, wrote hit songs, and produced Cash, Waylon Jennings, and Charley Pride, among others.

KENNY ROGERS

b. August 21, 1938; d. March 20, 2020 ▪ Houston, Texas

Kenny Rogers parlayed his distinctive, rough-around-the-edges voice and laid-back sex appeal into durable stardom across musical formats. After scoring hits with pop group the First Edition, Rogers turned to country music, enjoying twenty #1 country hits between 1977 and 1987. A star of film and TV, he sold more than fifty million albums worldwide.

2014

HANK COCHRAN

b. August 2, 1935; d. July 15, 2010 ▪ Isola, Mississippi

Hank Cochran helped create the template for the professional Nashville songwriter. Arriving in Music City in 1960, he joined a group of non-conformists who refined country songwriting and established Music City's reputation as a mecca for songwriters. His mastery of wordcraft and melody tapped into complex human behavior in everyday language, creating a string of classic songs that have stood the test of time.

RONNIE MILSAP

b. January 16, 1943 ▪ Robbinsville, North Carolina

Ronnie Milsap's emotionally expressive voice and broad musical talent made him one of the most consistent and enduring country artists in the 1970s and 1980s. Drawing on a diverse background in pop and R&B, as well as on classical music training, the blind pianist created an extensive string of hits during a time when country music was enjoying growing popularity and crossover success.

Maxine Brown, Becky Brown, Bonnie Brown Ring, and Bobby Bare at the 2015 Medallion Ceremony.

MAC WISEMAN

b. May 23, 1925; d. February 24, 2019 ▪ Crimora, Virginia

Mac Wiseman, with his expressive tenor voice and preference for sentimental songs, became known as "The Voice with a Heart"—one of country music's most accurate nicknames. The versatile singer and guitarist blended bluegrass, country, and folk into a long career that included stints as a producer, record executive, and member of the Country Music Association board of directors.

2015

JIM ED BROWN AND THE BROWNS

Formed 1952 in Little Rock, Arkansas

Jim Ed, Maxine, and Bonnie Brown were a successful vocal group—the Browns—of the Nashville Sound era. Their three-part harmonies influenced groups from the Beatles to the Whites. Jim Ed enjoyed a long career as a solo artist, with hits such as "Pop a Top," and he also recorded and performed as a duet partner with Helen Cornelius.

GRADY MARTIN

b. January 17, 1929; d. December 3, 2001 ▪ Marshall County, Tennessee

Grady Martin was a renowned member of Nashville's original "A-Team" of studio musicians. Whether playing fiddle or guitar—electric, acoustic, or six-string electric bass—his versatility and creativity in playing and arranging shaped numerous hits from the 1950s through the 1970s.

OAK RIDGE BOYS

William Lee Golden (joined in 1965); Duane Allen (1966); Richard Sterban (1972); Joe Bonsall (1973)

With roots in the gospel music of Wally Fowler's Oak Ridge Quartet, the Oak Ridge Boys achieved popular success by applying four-part harmonies to country songs and by entertaining crowds with a dynamic stage presence. Starting in 1977, the Oaks notched twenty-six Top Ten country hits, sold millions of albums, and won numerous awards.

Singing "Will the Circle Be Unbroken" at the conclusion of the 2016 Medallion Ceremony. Left to right: Charlie Daniels, Charley Pride, Joe Bonsall and William Lee Golden of the Oak Ridge Boys, and Randy Travis (seated).

2016

CHARLIE DANIELS

b. October 28, 1936; d. July 6, 2020 ▪ Wilmington, North Carolina

Charlie Daniels brought rock and blues motifs to mainstream country music. Forming the Charlie Daniels Band in 1971, Daniels sang, played guitar and fiddle, and wrote and recorded songs that reached the country and rock charts, including "The Devil Went Down to Georgia." He founded the recurring Volunteer Jam concert series in 1974.

FRED FOSTER

b. July 26, 1931; d. February 20, 2019 ▪ Rutherford County, North Carolina

As a record producer and the founder of Monument Records, Fred Foster played a crucial role in the careers of Jimmy Dean, Kris Kristofferson, Willie Nelson, Roy Orbison, Dolly Parton, Boots Randolph, Jeannie Seely, Ray Stevens, and others. Foster's publishing company, Combine Music, helped advance a gritty, literate form of songwriting.

RANDY TRAVIS

b. May 4, 1959 ▪ Marshville, North Carolina

Randy Travis ranked among the leaders of a group of young, tradition-minded artists who changed the course of country music in the 1980s. His 1986 debut album, *Storms of Life*, introduced his understated, hard-country baritone and square-jawed sex appeal. He also became a successful actor, appearing in more than thirty films.

2017

ALAN JACKSON

b. October 17, 1958 ▪ Newnan, Georgia

Alan Jackson built his reputation by finding fresh ways to update traditional styles while focusing on lyrics that tell personal stories, extol his values, and indulge his humor. Within time-tested country parameters, Jackson drew on a broad musical range in his recordings, including bluegrass, Cajun, honky-tonk, gospel, love ballads, tear-in-your-beer heartbreakers, and western swing.

JERRY REED

b. March 20, 1937; d. September 1, 2008 ▪ Atlanta, Georgia

Jerry Reed left an indelible mark on American music with his complex, fingerstyle guitar playing, his original songs, and a rambunctious, southern-bred attitude that shined through in his vocals and his stage performances. His distinctive guitar style influenced scores of other pickers. He also became an in-demand actor, appearing in successful films such as *Smokey and the Bandit* (1977) and *The Waterboy* (1998).

Alan Jackson and Loretta Lynn at the 2017 Medallion Ceremony.

DON SCHLITZ

b. August 29, 1952 ▪ Durham, North Carolina

Songwriter Don Schlitz created a voluminous body of work—including "The Gambler," "When You Say Nothing at All," and "Forever and Ever, Amen"—that presents an uncommon understanding of common situations. His songs feature an atypical perspective, an ever-present command of rhyme and meter, and an enduring and endearing empathy for the characters he creates

2018

JOHNNY GIMBLE

b. May 30, 1926; d. May 9, 2015 ▪ Tyler, Texas

Influential fiddle stylist Johnny Gimble contributed to country recordings for more than fifty years. A master of jazz-influenced improvisation, he had his fiddle modified with an additional fifth string, enabling him to produce lower, mellower tones. His career encompassed playing in Bob Wills's western swing band, *Hee Haw*'s Million Dollar Band of star musicians, and numerous Nashville recording sessions beginning in 1968.

RICKY SKAGGS

b. July 18, 1954 ▪ Cordell, Kentucky

A soaring tenor vocalist adept on the mandolin, guitar, and fiddle, Ricky Skaggs fine-tuned his craft in the bands of bluegrass patriarch Ralph Stanley and Emmylou Harris before becoming a solo artist. His eleven #1 country hits include "Heartbroke," "Uncle Pen," and "Country Boy." The CMA's 1985 Entertainer of the Year, he has been a force for maintaining the traditions of bluegrass.

DOTTIE WEST

b. October 11, 1932; d. September 4, 1991 ▪ McMinnville, Tennessee

The first artist to win a Grammy for Best Female Country Vocal Performance, Dottie West enjoyed a long career as a songwriter, hitmaker, and Grand Ole Opry star. She earned a Top Ten country hit and a Grammy with her song "Here Comes My Baby" (1964). She had ten more Top Ten records between 1964 and 1981, and recorded three #1 duets with Kenny Rogers.

2019

JERRY BRADLEY

b. January 30, 1940; d. July 17, 2023 ▪ Nashville, Tennessee

Music executive Jerry Bradley grew up in the business as the son of record producer and label executive Owen Bradley and nephew of studio guitarist Harold Bradley. Jerry headed RCA Nashville from 1973 to 1982 (during which he conceived the platinum compilation album *Wanted! The Outlaws*) and ran the music publishing firm Opryland Music Group until retirement in 2003.

Hall of Fame member Ricky Skaggs embraces the mandolin of his bluegrass hero, Bill Monroe, also a Hall of Fame member, 2018.

BROOKS & DUNN

Formed 1990 in Nashville, Tennessee

Kix Brooks from Louisiana and Ronnie Dunn from Texas achieved their destiny together in Tennessee as the best-selling country music duo of all time. Formerly solo artists, the two joined forces in 1990, writing songs together and recording them as a duo. They earned twenty #1 singles and sales of more than twenty-nine million records as of 2021.

RAY STEVENS

b. January 24, 1939 ▪ Clarkdale, Georgia

A singer, songwriter, session musician, arranger, and musical comedian, Ray Stevens arrived in Nashville in 1962, and a string of pop and country novelty hits quickly followed, including "Guitarzan," "The Streak," and "Shriner's Convention." His 1970 song "Everything Is Beautiful" was a #1 pop hit. It won him a Grammy and has become a modern standard.

2020

DEAN DILLON

b. March 26, 1955 ▪ Lake City, Tennessee

Songwriter extraordinaire Dean Dillon wrote with and for masters, eventually becoming a master himself. He supplied hits for top country artists, including Kenny Chesney, Toby Keith, and Chris Stapleton. Dillon wrote more than sixty songs for George Strait that defined both men's careers—from Strait's first hit single, "Unwound," to "The Chair," "Ocean Front Property," and "Easy Come Easy Go."

MARTY STUART

b. September 30, 1958 ▪ Philadelphia, Mississippi

Marty Stuart joined Lester Flatt's band at thirteen, landed a spot in Johnny Cash's band in 1980, and pursued a solo career in 1985. Stuart went on to become not only a revered musician and singer but also a songwriter, producer, photographer, television host, and spokesman for the history and traditions of the music that he holds so dear.

HANK WILLIAMS JR.

b. May 26, 1949 ▪ Shreveport, Louisiana

Hank Williams Jr. has bridged generations by mastering time-honored styles including rock and blues. The son of Country Music Hall of Fame member Hank Williams, Hank Jr. had his first charting single at age fourteen. Over the next five decades, he reached the charts more than one hundred times, with ten of those records reaching #1 on the country singles charts.

2021

EDDIE BAYERS

b. January 28, 1949 ▪ Patuxent River, Maryland

A top studio drummer of country music's modern era, Eddie Bayers began as a professional keyboardist. He shifted to drums and by the early 1980s established himself as leading Nashville session drummer. Along the way, he developed longstanding working relationships with many artists including the Judds, Ricky Skaggs, George Strait, Alan Jackson, and Kenny Chesney.

RAY CHARLES

b. September 23, 1930; d. June 10, 2004 ▪ Albany, Georgia

A pioneer of R&B, Ray Charles was also enormously influential in country music. With his landmark 1962 album *Modern Sounds in Country and Western Music*, the soulful singer and pianist put his own indelible stamp on country songs, broadening the music's appeal and audience. He made country music a significant part of his repertoire from that point forward.

PETE DRAKE

b. October 8, 1932; d. July 29, 1988 ▪ Augusta, Georgia

Pete Drake left a lasting mark on country music as a producer, music publisher, independent label owner, and especially as a premier pedal steel guitarist. A year after arriving in Nashville in 1959, he became a first-call session musician, playing on countless country hits. He also played pedal steel on major rock albums by Bob Dylan, George Harrison, and Elvis Presley.

Hank Williams Jr. kneels as Brenda Lee drapes his Hall of Fame Medallion around his neck during the 2021 Medallion Ceremony.

THE JUDDS

Formed 1979 in Franklin, Tennessee

The Judds—mother Naomi and daughter Wynonna—helped take country back to its roots in the 1980s with lean, tuneful songs influenced by folk music, blues, and family harmony acts. Wynonna sang with a husky, expressive voice, while Naomi provided blood harmonies and an engaging stage presence. Between 1984 and 1991, the Judds scored a remarkable twenty Top Ten hits.

2022

JOE GALANTE

b. December 18, 1949 ▪ Queens, New York

Joe Galante was one of country music's most successful record executives. He helped steer the careers of Alabama, Clint Black, Kenny Chesney, the Judds, Martina McBride, Carrie Underwood, and other best-selling artists during his four decades in the record business. He became the head of RCA Nashville in 1982 and ended his label career as chairman of Sony Music Nashville in 2010.

JERRY LEE LEWIS

b. September 29, 1935; d. October 28, 2022 ▪ Ferriday, Louisiana

An explosive rockabilly performer early in his career, Jerry Lee Lewis later became a major country star, with a distinctive and dynamic style as a singer and pianist. Between 1968 and 1981, he had thirty-four Top Twenty country hits, putting his personal stamp on songs ranging from classics by Jimmie Rodgers and Hank Williams to newer works by Mickey Newbury and Kris Kristofferson.

KEITH WHITLEY

b. July 1, 1954; d. May 9, 1989 ▪ Ashland, Kentucky

A premier vocal stylist, Keith Whitley helped define country music's new traditionalist resurgence of the 1980s. After apprenticing in bluegrass bands starting as a teenager, he signed with RCA Records. In five years, he recorded a dozen Top Twenty solo country singles, including five consecutive #1 hits. His career was cut tragically short at age thirty-four.

2023

PATTY LOVELESS

b. January 4, 1957 ▪ Pikeville, Kentucky

Like her distant cousin Loretta Lynn, Patty Loveless was a coal miner's daughter. Following a brief detour singing rock songs in bar bands, she pursued her true calling as a country recording artist starting in the mid-1980s. Between 1988 and 2003, she scored thirty-one Top Twenty country hits, including the #1s "Timber, I'm Falling in Love," "Blame It on Your Heart," and "Lonely Too Long."

At the 2023 Medallion Ceremony, Tanya Tucker (center) exults in her induction with Hall of Fame friends Connie Smith (left) and Brenda Lee.

BOB McDILL

b. April 5, 1944 ▪ Beaumont, Texas

Bob McDill approached songwriting like a skilled craft or trade, and produced some of country music's most artful and enduring songs. Between 1972 and his retirement in 2000, he wrote numerous #1 country hits, including "Amanda," "Don't Close Your Eyes," "Gone Country," and "Good Ole Boys Like Me." Don Williams alone recorded more than thirty McDill songs, fourteen of them hits.

TANYA TUCKER

b. October 10, 1958 ▪ Seminole, Texas

A hit recording artist at age thirteen and a millionaire at sixteen, Tanya Tucker grew up fast. Powered by her husky voice and often adult-themed songs ("Delta Dawn," "Blood Red and Going Down"), she landed six #1 records before she turned eighteen. Following an unsatisfying flirtation with pop-rock and a three-year recording hiatus, she scored twenty-four Top Ten country hits from 1986 to 1997.

2024

JOHN ANDERSON

b. December 13, 1954 ▪ Apopka, Florida

John Anderson made an enduring impact in country music with his down-home, instantly recognizable singing style and memorable recordings. Influenced by Merle Haggard, George Jones, Lefty Frizzell, and Levon Helm of the Band, Anderson fashioned his own breathy, note-bending vocal approach, putting a distinctive stamp on hard-country ballads ("Wild and Blue") and uptempo numbers ("Seminole Wind") alike.

JAMES BURTON

b. August 21, 1939 ▪ Dubberly, Louisiana

Few guitarists have shaped the sounds of country music—and popular music—more than James Burton. At eighteen, he led Ricky Nelson's band, where he crafted influential rockabilly licks and solos. As a session musician, he backed artists ranging from Merle Haggard to the Beach Boys. He then led Elvis Presley's band, followed by long stints backing Emmylou Harris, John Denver, and others.

TOBY KEITH

b. July 8, 1961; d. February 5, 2024 ▪ Clinton, Oklahoma

For nearly thirty years, Toby Keith was a leading star in country music, racking up forty-two Top Ten country hits and twenty #1 hits. Keith wrote or co-wrote most of his material, sharing a perspective that was by turns tough, tender, and humorous in songs such as "Courtesy of the Red, White and Blue," "Hope on the Rocks," and "As Good as I Once Was."

2025

TONY BROWN

b. December 11, 1946 ▪ Greensboro, North Carolina

A former keyboard player in the bands of Elvis Presley and Emmylou Harris, Tony Brown became a key record executive in country music. As a producer, he supervised recordings by Country Music Hall of Fame members Vince Gill, Wynonna Judd, Patty Loveless, Reba McEntire, George Strait, Marty Stuart, and others. As a label executive, he brought daring talents into mainstream country music, including Steve Earle and Lyle Lovett.

JUNE CARTER CASH

b. June 23, 1929; d. May 15, 2003 ▪ Maces Springs, Virginia

June Carter Cash was a vibrant presence in country music for over sixty years as a singer, comedienne, and songwriter. With her mother, Maybelle Carter, and her two sisters she starred on the Grand Ole Opry and in Johnny Cash's roadshow. She wrote "Ring of Fire," a #1 hit for Cash, whom she married in 1968. They recorded several hit duets, including "Jackson."

KENNY CHESNEY

b. March 26, 1968 ▪ Knoxville, Tennessee

Kenny Chesney parlayed a resonant baritone voice and a dynamic stage presence into one of the biggest careers in country music in the 2000s. He has earned sixteen platinum albums, more than fifty Top Ten country hits, and twenty-three #1s on *Billboard*'s Hot Country Songs chart. A perennial top touring attraction, he's been voted the CMA Entertainer of the Year four times—2004, 2006, 2007, and 2008. ■

Singing "Will the Circle Be Unbroken" at the conclusion of the 2017 Medallion Ceremony.
Left to right: George Strait, Loretta Lynn, Connie Smith, and Alan Jackson.
Opposite page: Don Schlitz's typewriter